D1126427

ETHICS AND ECONOMIC PROGRESS

Ethics and
Economic Progress

By James M. Buchanan

UNIVERSITY OF OKLAHOMA : NORMAN AND LONDON

OTHER BOOKS BY JAMES M. BUCHANAN

(with Gordon Tullock) *The Calculus of Consent: Logical Foundations of Constitutional Democracy* (Ann Arbor, 1962)
The Limits of Liberty: Between Anarchy and Leviathan (Chicago, 1975)
Freedom in Constitutional Contract (College Station, Texas, 1978)
Liberty, Market, and State: Political Economy in the 1980s (Brighton, 1985)
Economics: Between Predictive Science and Moral Philosophy (College Station, Texas, 1987)
The Economics and the Ethics of Constitutional Order (Ann Arbor, 1991)
Better than Plowing and Other Personal Essays (Chicago, 1992)

Library of Congress Cataloging-in-Publication Data
Buchanan, James M.
    Ethics and economic progress / by James M. Buchanan.
      p. cm.
    Includes bibliographical references and index.
    ISBN 0–8061–2596–9
    1. Economics—Moral and ethical aspects. 2. Work ethic.
    3. Economic development—Moral and ethical aspects. I. Title.
    HB72.B833   1994
    174'.4—dc20
                                 93–31846
                                       CIP

The paper in this book meets the guidelines for permanence and durability of the Committee on Production Guidelines for Book Longevity of the Council on Library Resources, Inc. ∞

18223

1 2 3 4 5 6 7 8 9 10

Contents

Preface   vii

PART I   THREE LECTURES   I
         Chapter 1.   We Should All Work More:
                      The Economic Value of the
                      Work Ethic   5
         Chapter 2.   We Should All Save More: The
                      Economics of the Saving Ethic   31
         Chapter 3.   We Should All Pay the
                      Preacher: The Economic
                      Origins of Ethical Constraints   60

PART II THREE PAPERS ON THE THEME   89
         Chapter 4.   Externality in Tax Response   91
         Chapter 5.   The Economics and the Ethics
                      of Idleness   112
         Chapter 6.   The Simple Economics of the
                      Menial Servant   129

References   147
Index   151

Preface

There are two parts to this book. The first part contains the revised texts of three lectures presented at the University of Oklahoma in October 1991. The lectures are on a single theme that is summarized in the book's title, *Ethics and Economic Progress*. The second part contains three chapters written separately which are closely related to the central theme. Two of these chapters were written for presentation as lectures at St. John's University, George Mason University, and the Southern Economic Association and have not been published. The third chapter, "Externality in Tax Response," was published in 1966 in the *Southern Economic Journal* and has not been previously reprinted. At the time that I wrote it, I did not recognize the generalization of the argument that becomes possible once analysis is shifted out of the neoclassical paradigm embodying universal constant returns. In one sense, the chapter might be used as an introduction to the more complex arguments in the other chapters of the book.

The argument of chapter 1 relating to the work ethic has been developed over several stages of sophistication. Earlier versions have appeared. A short summary sketch of the analysis was published in my small book *Essays on the Political Economy* (Honolulu: University of Hawaii Press, 1989). A somewhat more complete but still informal argument was published as a single chapter in my book *The Economics and the Ethics of Constitutional Order* (Ann Arbor: University of Michigan Press, 1991). And a more complex and formal variant of the argument, jointly written with Yong J. Yoon, will be published in an edited volume, *The Return to Increasing Returns* (Ann Arbor: University of Michigan Press, forthcoming). The presentation in lecture form included here is, however, quite substantively different from the alternative efforts.

An early, very different version of the argument in chapter 3 is also included in *The Economics and the Ethics of Constitutional Order*.

The most controversial argument is probably that presented in chapter 6, where I suggest that Adam Smith's distinction between productive and unproductive labor has more merit than it is normally granted by modern economic theorists. I limit discussion to the labor of menial servants, but it is clear that the argument could be very considerably extended to apply to many other categories of employment. I should like, in particular, to extend the analysis to labor employed in the production of many services, especially those that are supplied collectively or through governmental auspices. This statement of intent suggests that the analysis opened up by this book's central theme is by no means closed or complete.

ACKNOWLEDGMENTS

I should, first of all, express my appreciation to the University of Oklahoma, especially through the offices of Dean Rufus Fears of the College of Arts and Sciences, for inviting me to present the lectures in 1991 and, indirectly, to W. R. Howell, whose support made the lecture series possible.

For my own part in the production process, I have relied, as on so many previous occasions, on my long-time assistant-agent, Betty Tillman. And I must also acknowledge the help of Jo Ann Burgess, whose skills with modern technology continue to confound me. I should also extend these remarks to include Yong J. Yoon, whose support and assistance in formalizing some of the analysis has, indirectly, shored up my confidence in the whole enterprise.

I acknowledge the permission of the *Southern Economic Journal* to reprint, as chapter 4, a revised version of an earlier paper.

JAMES M. BUCHANAN

Fairfax, Virginia

PART I
THREE LECTURES

Part I contains three chapters on closely related themes, which may be summarized under the generalized title, "Ethics and Economic Progress," or, less inclusively, "The Economics of Ethics," or, even more descriptively, "The Economic Value of Ethical Norms." As these titles may suggest, the subject matter reflects my disciplinary qualifications; the core discipline here is economics, not ethics. The central thesis is straightforward. Ethical or moral constraints on human behavior exert important economic effects, measured in positive or negative economic values. From this thesis emerges the implication that because such constraints exert economic effects, ethical norms or principles are relevant determinants of the welfare of all persons who share membership in an economic nexus. Standards of well-being of any person are, in part, the result of how other persons behave in an ethical or moral sense, from which it follows that some sets of ethical precepts or principles are "better" than others, if we use "better" in terms of welfare as ultimately measured by the individuals' own preferences.

Even within the limits that may be suggested by the titles mentioned above, however, my subject matter must be restricted. I surely do not propose to take on the task of evaluating all sets of ethical principles to analyze their potential economic content, whether this content may be judged positive, neutral, or negative in effect. My purpose is much more confined. Specifically, I shall analyze and discuss only a few familiar ethical standards, all of which might be summarized under the rubric "Puritan ethics." Hence, an even more descriptive but still inclusive title for part I might be "The Economic Value of Puritan Ethical Norms," with the proviso that most of us share a common understanding of the adjective "Puritan" in this context. I have hesitated to use this title, however, since I do not want to enter into theological, historical, or interpretive disputation concerning the extent to which the descriptive adjective "Puritan," in the meaning sought here, corresponds or fails to correspond to the teachings of this or that set of religious institutions or creeds, then or now. That is to say, I am not interested in the question of whether Max Weber (1930) was right or wrong in his famous attribution of the capitalistic spirit to Protestant, especially Calvinistic, ethics. (See chap. 3, sec. VII, for further discussion.) Instead, I want, simply, to take the most familiar norms that we associate with the term "Puritan ethics" and subject them to economic analysis.

In chapter 1, I shall examine the work ethic in some detail. I hope that I shall be able to offer a convincing argument to the effect that "working harder" or "working more" can be, and is, good for all of us, "good" in terms of our own preferences, whatever these may be, and totally divorced from any externally derived criteria for "goodness," whether from the self-anointed philosophers or from the presumed dictates of some transcendental deity.

The second chapter extends the argument to the saving
ethic. In one sense, the argument here has more immediate
and important practical implications than those that might
be drawn from chapter 1. While I may convince you that we
should all "work more," it remains, nonetheless, factually
correct to say that something like a work ethic remains
empirically descriptive of much of our everyday behavioral
routines. In dramatic contrast, there seems to be general
agreement, in both scientific and public opinion, that we
have allowed the saving ethic to become seriously eroded,
as it is indirectly reflected in both our public and private
choice processes. As the discussion in the second chapter
will indicate, however, despite the more general opinion
that something may be amiss with respect to our willingness to save and to invest, the argument that we should all
save more, in our own economic interest, is somewhat more
complex than that which relates to the norms for work.

The third chapter is categorically different from the first
two in that it does not examine a particular behavioral
attribute directly. It is, nonetheless, a natural follow-on or
extension to the discussion-analysis of chapters 1 and 2. If,
indeed, we are all better off in an environment where we
work hard and save, it follows that "preaching" such
virtues, that is, inculcating these norms in others — and in
society generally — yields positive returns that can be conceptually measured in economic value. Hence, investment
in the transmission of such norms becomes a part of an
overall rational calculus, on the part of each and every
individual. These "Puritan" norms that yield positive
returns must, of course, be sharply distinguished from
those ethical-moral precepts that are perhaps much more
observed in modern discourse, those that may promise
negative payoffs when evaluated economically. The argument in chapter 3 suggests that we should all "pay the

preacher," on strictly economic grounds, but only if that which is preached is what we find to be of ultimate value to us, as opposed to the value-reducing or value-destroying norms of altruism and indulgence shouted from modern pulpits. (I should add that any treatment of noneconomic bases for "paying the preacher" is beyond my ken.)

The lectures were presented to general academic audiences that included noneconomists. In both the oral presentations and in this written version, I have tried to avoid technical economic analysis, as such. At the same time, I should say that the central argument is by no means within the corpus of conventional modern economics. My purpose is the catholic one of convincing both economists and noneconomists that the analysis is correct and that the policy implications are important. Not surprisingly perhaps, the noneconomists may be more readily converted than the economists; professional specialization tends to harden mind-sets.

Chapter 1

We Should All Work Harder: The Economic Value of the Work Ethic

I. INTRODUCTION

Members of a society in which there is a strong work ethic will be better off, materially, than those of a society in which any such ethic is weak or nonexistent. This statement will be accepted without question by persons who do not classify themselves as professional economists. By contrast, economists will find the statement difficult to incorporate into their analytical orthodoxy. Why is a person, any person, better off, in terms of his or her own evaluation, if those with whom interaction in an economy takes place work harder? What is there in basic economic theory that will enable us to ground the logic of the basic intuition here?

These are the questions that prompted my initial

inquiry. In section II, I provide the autobiographical details. Section III puts the questions in a form amenable to careful economic analysis by making the minimal clarifying and definitional assumptions. In section IV, Adam Smith's classical principle that relates the division of labor to the extent of the market is adduced to offer a straightforward response. But, as the discussion in section V suggests, this response may not be consistent with the neoclassical principle of distribution, which is also a part of the received wisdom. In section VI, I resolve the apparent contradiction by dropping the constant-returns postulate from the analysis of the production-exchange economy. The introduction of generalized or economywide increasing returns allows for a logical grounding of the initial intuition, although the optimality properties of competitive equilibrium are called into some question.

If there does, indeed, exist an externality at the work-leisure margin of choice, how might such a potential source of inefficiency be internalized? Section VII suggests that internalization by way of ethical norms may have offered at least a partial resolution. In this section and in the final section of the chapter, I argue that there is demonstrable economic constant in a work ethic, that the noneconomists' initial intuition may be analytically supported, on the basis of applying Smith's principle in a setting of generalized increasing returns, and that, in one sense, the presence of a work ethic in our cultural heritage may, indeed, reflect an indirect recognition of the relationship.

II. FOOTBALL AND WALNUTS:
A PERSONAL STORY

I shall commence my discussion of the work ethic by relating the origins of my own interest, a personal story that I have told in earlier versions of the argument (see Buchanan 1989). Those who know something of my career path will recognize that the specific research program in the economics of ethics is a relatively recent development of my interests. This program did not emerge directly from the public choice, political philosophy, or constitutional economics emphases of my earlier work, although there are obvious intersections, especially with the latter.

On the weekend of January 3 and 4, 1987, four professional football playoff games were scheduled. I enjoy watching professional football on television, and my preferences strongly suggested that I watch all four of these games. But I felt very guilty about planning to sit on the couch for some fifteen hours on a single weekend. I was very upset at the prospective "waste" of valued time.

I was in my country house in the Virginia mountains, and I recalled that a few weeks earlier I had collected a good crop of black walnuts from a tree in my garden. As you may know, black walnuts make delicious nutmeats for candies and cakes, but they are very hard nuts to crack (indeed, these nuts may have offered the origins of this American idiom). But, as it turned out, the black walnuts were the answer to my prayers. I hit onto the idea of getting some bowls, nutpicks, a hammer, and an ancient flatiron to put on my lap and cracking the walnuts while watching the many hours of football. In the process of the two-day adventure, I accumulated several jars of nutmeats, which made any market purchase of this item unnecessary. And I found, to my surprise, that the work of shelling the walnuts assuaged my guilt about watching football on television. I was, of course, enjoying the spectacle; but I was, at the same time, engaging in something less than totally "wasteful" activity.

It was the process of examining my own psyche both during and after this event that initiated my inquiry into the economic content of the work ethic. Clearly, I was constrained by an internal ethical principle that made it very painful to respond to my own preferences. I felt a genuine sense of guilt when the prospect of almost pure "loafing" appeared, a sense that remains with me on all like occasions. But this guilt was removed quickly when some work became possible, even work that was well beyond the normal activities of my existence (and which, of course, in a comparative advantage sense remained "noneconomic").

Query: Is this deeply embedded ethical precept, perhaps present in part due to my upbringing in a Scots-Irish, middle Tennessee, Presbyterian heritage, simply a carry-over of a trait that in some earlier epoch may have been necessary for survival in a subsistence setting, hence a trait that carries no meaning or value in the complex modern economy? Or, perhaps, does

WE SHOULD ALL WORK MORE   9

this ethic of work, which clearly directs me to counter my own preferences for nonwork on occasion, retain economic meaning and value, even in the economy of the late twentieth century?

III. CLARIFYING THE QUESTION

The question is challenging, but before commencing the search for an answer, it is necessary to put on the professional economist's hat and pose the question in an abstracted model that is designed to isolate the relevant features. Generally put, the question is, are participants in an economy better off when they share an ethical commitment to work hard than they are when they share no such commitment? As my title for this chapter suggests, I shall answer this question in the affirmative, but I must mount a convincing argument in support.

There is a commonsense meaning of "more work" that embodies several dimensions of adjustment: hours, days, weeks, months, years of work; rate of output per time unit, per hour, per day, per week, and so on; quality of work effort as measured by quality of output and by others. To simplify the question, I shall concentrate here on the time dimension alone. By a choice to work more, I shall refer to an individual's choice of more hours per week, weeks per year, or years per career. I shall assume that the rate per time unit is not changed over varying times worked, and also I shall assume that the quality of work is invariant over

differing times worked. Further, I shall assume that
the individual is not institutionally constrained along
his or her work time dimension; that is, I assume that
the individual can choose voluntarily the number of
hours per week, weeks per year, or years per career
worked. Realistically, of course, there are many institutional constraints that restrict voluntary choice of
work time, such as stipulated hours per week, weeks
per year, retirement ages, and so on. But, in almost all
cases, individuals do have some aspects of the time
dimension that remain within their own choice set.

I have now reduced the question to the following:
Are participants in an economy better off if they share a
common ethical precept that causes them to work more
hours per week or more weeks per year than they would
be without such a precept? As a next step, it is
necessary to define carefully just what is involved in a
choice to put in more working time. My definition in
this respect is quite straightforward and is strictly in
accordance with normal usage of terms. When a person
puts in more working time, when he or she extends the
number of hours worked per week, there is a corre-
sponding increase in the payment, the wage or salary,
received as income by the work supplier. The individual produces more economic value for whomever em-
ploys him or her and in return for this increase in value
of input supplied, receives an increase in the total wage
or salary, which is then available for spending as the
recipient so desires on final goods and services in the
economy.

The definition of just what is meant by more working time seems clear, but it does rule out much that we might carelessly refer to as work. The definition restricts the meaning of more work to more time offered in exchange for a wage or salary payment in the market. The individual who "works hard" or "spends more hours" improving his golf or tennis game is not increasing the supply of effort to the economic nexus. Hence, for our purposes, spending more time on golf is equivalent to spending more time as a couch potato. The critical margin is that between the supply of labor to the market and all other uses of an individual's time. To an individual, of course, the time spent perfecting a golf game may yield value that is equal to or above that value of the goods that might be purchased by the wage or salary income from the comparable time offered to the market. But the individual places value on the market, which might be of potential value to others, only as and when he supplies input to the market.

A final qualification to the analysis may be required for full clarification. I assume that the institutions of the overall economy, sometimes called the macroeconomic institutions, are operative in such a fashion that allows the voluntary choices of persons concerning the supplies of work effort to be carried out without institutional breakdown. Since the individual who supplies work to the market receives, in return, income that can, in principle, purchase the value of output that is equal to the value of input supplied, any observed inability of the aggregate economy to absorb changes in the supply of work must be traced directly to institutional failure, which can, presumably, be corrected. Any argument to the effect that, because there is only so much demand for labor, any increase in supply must create unemployment is surely specious and does not deserve extended treatment here. I shall leave the discussion of institutional arrangements necessary for macroaggregate stability to those who classify themselves as macroeconomists. (See chap. 2, sec. III, for further discussion.)

IV. THE DIVISION OF LABOR AND THE EXTENT OF THE MARKET

I apologize for the tedious detour into definitions and qualifications. It is time to get on with the substantive argument. As clarified, the question now concerns the value of more work, or more work than our naked preferences might dictate. Are we better off when we all work harder? Or, to state the same thing differently, why should I be concerned at all with how much you work or, indeed, with how much anyone else works?

When confronted with a question like this, my procedure is to examine the possible contribution that standard economic theory might make toward an answer. Like many economists, for me such an inquiry involves two steps. I try to recall what Adam Smith might have said about the question, and then I look at what modern textbooks say. And whereas Smith is quite clear on the subject, modern textbooks seem, perhaps surprisingly, to offer conflicting and contradictory responses.

Let me first concentrate on Adam Smith. In his great book, *The Wealth of Nations*, published in 1776, he located and identified the primary source of an economy's (or a nation's) productivity as the effective exploitation of the division or specialization of labor. Even if, as Smith himself believed, persons differ relatively little in their basic abilities to produce economic value, they can greatly enhance their productivity if they specialize, that is, if different persons do different things. Overall, much more value can be generated in an economy where different persons, or groups of persons, produce different goods and then exchange these goods among themselves.

Imagine, as a mental exercise, what it would be like to try to produce everything on your own, with no economic interaction with others. How much could a person produce in total independence from any exchange nexus? A person's life would indeed be solitary, nasty, brutish, and short, to use Thomas Hobbes's description in a different context. We might want to add the word "tiring," since the valued output that would be secured from the maximal inputs of labor would scarcely ensure survival.

The potted history of the American West, stripped of some of the romance, offers us a good basis for thinking about the benefits of the division of labor and exchange. An isolated homestead on the frontier was, by necessity, forced to be self-sufficient in many of its activities. But this genuine independence from others, this home production, was purchased at the price of a very low standard of creature comforts. As other families moved closer to the isolated homestead and a town took shape, specialization increased. And productivity was dramatically enhanced because persons could devote full or almost full time to single activities. Even after the establishment of a town, however, in the early years, the same person might serve as barber and surgeon, as we know from the Western films. Even this arrangement was much more productive than that which required each family to perform these services along with others. But as the town grew in size, as the economic nexus expanded, productivity again increased as and when barbers and surgeons found their custom sufficient to specialize.

The whole technology of production shifts as specialization proceeds and as the number of suppliers, and demanders, increases. In the historical record that we know, innovations in transportation and communication both preceded and followed increases in specialization. Individuals and families came to accept the complex interlinkage of a wide market nexus as a natural phenomenon. In today's setting, a person devotes almost no attention to his or her almost total dependence on all of the other persons who participate in the market, far and near. A person expects to be able to sell his or her own resources, by far the most important resource being labor time, for a salary, wage, or other type of payment and, further, expects to be able to purchase the bundle of goods most desired at the local supermarket or store. The family in today's economy is such a socioeconomic distance from the family on the frontier that an understanding of the historical process, even as an idea, is not within the ordinary mind-set.

When and if we consider the conjectural history, however, there is no reason to think that the advantages of specialization and division of labor come to be exhausted at some particular size of the network of interdependence. Smith advanced, as a general principle, the notion that the division of labor depends on the extent of the market. Why should any market network, therefore, go beyond that size at which further specialization fails to offer economic advantages?

If we acknowledge the nonexhaustibility of the advantages of specialization, we can then apply Smith's basic proposition directly to the question posed earlier. What happens when we work harder, when we supply more hours of work per week to the market in exchange for an increase in the take-home wage packet, which we then turn around and spend for an increased quantity of goods and services? The answer is obvious: We increase the *size* of the market, the network of economic interchange. If, for illustration, a person doubles the number of hours per week that he works and takes home a paycheck twice as large as before, which enables him to purchase a bundle of goods and services two times as valuable as before, his action is, in all respects, equivalent to the addition of another person to the exchange nexus, a person who has precisely the same capacities.

This direct linkage between the supplies of inputs, in our example, hours of labor, to the market and the size of the market itself allows us to make the connection between work effort and the advantages of specialization. More hours of work per week supplied to the market means a larger market, and a larger market means that specialization can be extended further, with generalized increases in the productivity of the whole economy. Hence, I am, indeed, made better off, in my own reckoning, if others in the economy work more, for the simple reason that my own inputs, no matter how many I choose to supply, will ultimately purchase a larger quantity of outputs than would be the case if other persons should supply fewer hours to the market.

Think of a simple mental experiment. Imagine yourself in a spaceship faced with landing, as a permanent resident, on either one of two planets, A and B. These planets have economies that are organized through markets, with similar characteristics such as population and natural resources but with one major difference. On Planet A, persons, on average, work forty hours per week. On Planet B, by comparison, persons, on average, work only twenty hours per week. Which of the two planets would you choose? If you consider only your economic advantage, it is evident that you would choose to become a participant in the economy on Planet A, where persons work more, for the simple reason that, no matter how much work you, yourself, supply to the market, the value of output purchasable per unit of input is higher than on Planet B. Specialization is extended further because the economy is larger; technology that is applicable on Planet A cannot be utilized on Planet B. Any end item of consumption, say, a pencil, might require, say, a minute's worth of work time on Planet A, whereas it might require three minutes' worth of work time on Planet B.

V. COMPETITIVE EQUILIBRIUM
AND CONSTANT RETURNS

To me, Adam Smith's argument is totally convincing. And, to be fair here to my fellow economists, let me add that almost all economists would accept the argument as presented to this point. Indeed, in the opening chapters of most elementary textbooks, we find references to the advantages of economic interdependence. The productivity gains from the division and specialization of resources in wide market networks are emphasized. In the implications that may be drawn from them, these introductory elements of economics do not conflict with Smith's basic proposition.

As I noted, however, the corpus of standard economic theory offers contradictory responses to the question at issue here. In chapter 1, as indicated, the textbook inference is yes, we should all be better off if we work more and for the reasons outlined above. But when we turn forward in the textbook, say, to an illustrative "chapter 17," we find quite a different story. At this point, the conventional analytical wisdom seems to embody a rejection of Smith's proposition. The discussion in "chapter 17" suggests that we cannot be made better off by working harder than our individual preferences dictate; the analysis suggests that a work ethic, as such, has no economic content. I use the metaphorical *"chapter 17"* to refer to the theory of distribution in standard economics. And here, a brief summary of the history of economic ideas may be useful.

Adam Smith and his fellow classical economists did not develop a fully acceptable theory of distribution. Within limits, they were able to develop a theory of resource allocation and a theory of value. They argued that relative prices are linked to relative costs of production and that departures from "natural prices" set in motion forces that work toward restoration of cost-price relationships. The self-interests of persons interact to promote an allocation of resources that tends to maximize the well-being of all participants. But, in one sense, the classical economists tried to push their cost of production theory of value too far. They tried to extend the explanatory logic to distribution. They sought to explain payments made to labor by the cost of producing workers, with the resultant subsistence theory of wages, on which Karl Marx constructed his familiar exploitation thesis.

The classical economists failed to recognize that relative prices depend not only on costs of production but also on the ultimate evaluations of persons, as expressed at the margins of usage, that is, on the marginal utilities that the goods were expected to provide. The classical economists offered a one-sided explanation of economic value when they placed exclusive reliance on costs of production to the neglect of marginal utilities. Had they been able to bring in the utility or demand side of an economic calculus, they would have noted that for some goods and some resources there may be little or no linkage between costs and market prices and that divergences between costs and prices do not always set in motion forces that tend to restore some determinate cost-price relationship.

The basic explanatory model that incorporates both the cost or supply and the demand side into the theory of value and allocation was introduced in the 1870s in the contributions of the neoclassical economists, sometimes called the subjective value or marginal utility theorists. And in the neoclassical model, the payments made to labor need not be directly related to the costs of producing workers. The distribution of income in an economy can be explained without introducing an economic theory of population. Workers, along with the suppliers of other inputs, or units of productive resources, tend to be paid in accordance with the contributions to value made by their employment. The marginal productivity theory of distribution becomes a theory of the pricing of inputs, or resource services, whether labor or other productive resources. Workers tend to be paid the value of the addition to final product value that they provide in their employment, and self-interest motivations ensure that similar workers get similar wages in all employments. And, importantly, input prices, like output prices, are set at the appropriate margins. Workers tend to get the value of their contribution to product value, at the margin of input usage. The wage of a single worker tends to be equal to the value that is added by his or her employment.

This theory of distribution, or theory of resource payments, is, of course, based on the presumption that the market order is fully operative. That is to say, competition in both input and output markets is assumed to be open, with no political or institutional restrictions on entry or exit into or from any occupation, any industry, any association.

The neoclassical theory of distribution, the theory of marginal productivity, seemed to be complete, but there remained a bit of a problem. If all input units, all units of resource that add to the value of the final product, should be paid in accordance with their net contribution to final product value, what is there to ensure that the total value of product is enough to go around, is just right, or if it is more than enough, who is to get the surplus? This "adding up" problem was solved by the second generation of neoclassical economists (J. B. Clark, P. Wicksteed, K. Wicksell) during the last decade of the nineteenth century. By specifying that production takes place under *constant returns*, that is, if a proportionate increase in all inputs occurs, an equiproportionate increase in output results, a mathematically unassailable proof exists demonstrating that the total product is precisely exhausted when each input is assigned its own marginal contribution to total output. Hence, under constant returns to scales of production, the competitive market equilibrium, which does tend to reward inputs in accordance with marginal productivity, allocates resources to their most highly valued uses, as evaluated by users of final product, and also assigns distributive shares among inputs owners in such a fashion as to use up all value that is generated in the economy.

This neoclassical construction is both powerful in an explanatory sense and aesthetically beautiful. The model suggests that to the extent that competitive markets are allowed to operate, as restricted only by the necessary laws that protect property and enforce contracts, the economic welfare of all participants in the economy is maximized, given any initial distribution of endowments, talents, and skills. Furthermore, when we think of productive activities separately, the constant returns requirement does not seem at all counterintuitive. If all inputs in a given line of production are expanded proportionately, should it not almost definitionally follow that output will also expand in equal proportion, within a given technology? But this neoclassical construction does not allow for change in the size of the whole economy, in the network of exchange, and hence for the necessary shifts in technology of production that such size changes might generate. That is to say, the neoclassical theory of economic interaction tells us nothing at all about the effects of changes in the overall or inclusive size of the economy, which, as noted above, is precisely what happens when there is an increase in the supply of labor inputs to the market.

If considered naively, the neoclassical construction seems to contradict Smith's basic proposition. Think of the following mental experiment. One person increases the number of hours worked per week; the supply of inputs to the market is increased. After full adjustments, this person receives precisely the value of the addition to the value of product that the extra work generates. The national product increases, to be sure, but *all* of the increase in value returns to the person whose additional work made the increase take place. From this line of reasoning, it seems to follow directly that no one else in the whole economy is affected, one way or the other, by the shift in the work habits of the person who makes the change. For me, then, it would seem that I should remain indifferent, at least in any economic calculus, as to whether you (or anyone else, or everyone else) work more or less hours. It would seem, by this logic, that loafing is strictly your own affair. Indeed, in strict economic terms, I should be unconcerned about having you in the economy at all.

This seemingly plausible inference from the standard neoclassical model is surely wrong, and the source of the error is readily located. The whole construction is based on the presumption of fixity in the supply of inputs, a presumption that is possibly derivative from some implicit notion that labor supply, overall, is measured by the number of warm bodies in the work force and is not affected by voluntary individual choices to work more or less. In this context, a work ethic is simply meaningless. With a given supply of inputs, overall, any increase in the supply for one productive activity must be matched by a decrease in the supply for some other activity. The size of the economy, as determined by the quantities of inputs supplied to the market, determines the technology of production, as described by the degree of specialization that is potentially utilized. There is simply no further scope for specialization within a given network size.

The inapplicability of the basic neoclassical model for the question at issue here should be clear. An increase in the supply of work to the market increases the size of the economy; hence, the whole explanatory construction that depends critically on a specification of fixity in resource supplies yields little or no insight. The contradiction in textbook analysis is apparent rather than real. There is no necessary inconsistency between the explanatory model of neoclassical economics, within its own assumptions, and Smith's proposition to the effect that an increase in the size of the market allows for increased specialization in resource use, which, in turn, increases the productivity of all inputs.

VI. OPTIMALITY, EXTERNALITY,
AND INCREASING RETURNS

In arguing that the economic welfare of each participant in a production-exchange economy depends in a
positive way on the work supply of others in the
economy, I am challenging, in one sense, a fundamental theorem in neoclassical economics concerning the
optimality properties of competitive market organization, even in its idealized form. As I have noted above,
I do not challenge this conventional wisdom within the
confines of the assumptions of resource and technological fixity. But I do call into question the implicit
presumption that the supply of inputs to the market
nexus remains somehow outside the domain of a rational choice calculus. And if the choice margin between
work supplied to the market and nonwork uses of
inputs (time) is introduced, my argument suggests
that individual voluntary adjustments need not generate results that are optimal or efficient, as defined in
the conventional Pareto way. That is to say, I suggest
that an economy in which all persons simply allow
their naked preferences to dictate their choices between work and nonwork will not be efficient and that
all persons can be made better off, by their own
reckoning, by a scheme that involves an increased
supply of work on the part of everyone.

There is an externality in the work-leisure choice.
The individual's choice to work more generates external benefits to others; the individual's choice to work

less generates external harms to others. More work involves spillover benefits to everyone; loafing generates spillover damages.

At this point, the neoclassical economist may raise objection to my argument. How can a change in one person's work supply to the market possibly exert a beneficial or harmful effect on others? In order for such external effects to exist, it is necessary to drop the presumption of constant returns and to postulate, instead, the presence of increasing returns. But increasing returns to the *size* of the whole network of exchange, to the size of the economy as measured by quantities of inputs supplied to the nexus, is precisely what Smith's basic proposition is about. An increase in the supply of inputs will generate a disproportionately larger increase in the value of total product because new technologies of production become possible only through the enhanced specialization that the increase in market size makes possible.

Care must be taken to distinguish between increasing returns to *scale* in any single production process and increasing returns to *size* of the whole economy, as measured by quantities of inputs employed. The neoclassical presumption of universalized constant returns to scale in all production processes may not be inconsistent with the presence of increasing returns to size of the whole economy, returns that are actuated only by a shift in technology. Nor need the neoclassical theory of distribution be substantially affected by a recognition of the presence of economywide increasing returns.

Within the presumptions of given resources and given technology, inputs owners are paid the values of the marginal products of inputs supplied, and, when added up, these payments fully exhaust the total value generated in the economy in full competitive equilibrium. The shift of an input unit away from one productive process tends to reduce the value of product in that process by the payment made to that unit, on the implicit presumption that the input *shifts to an alternative process that produces for the market*. The implied presumption is necessary to ensure that the effective size of the market, and hence the technology of specialization, remains unchanged.[1]

VII. INTERNALIZATION VIA THE WORK ETHIC

Let me return to my initial query: Does the existence of a work ethic have any economic content? I have argued

[1]Several of the propositions advanced in this paragraph depend critically on the assumed presence of severely restricted conditions. In order for increasing returns to the size of the whole economy to exist simultaneously with constant returns to all subsectors of the economy, the new technology consequent on the expansion in the size of the whole production-exchange nexus must apply to all subsectors. If, instead, the specialization technology made possible by the expansion in the size of the economy should differentially affect a subsector (a single industry or group of industries), increasing returns would, of course, characterize expansion in this subsector, even if implemented at the expense of reductions in the size of other sectors. If, however, all subsectors are roughly symmetrical with respect to the potential utilization of technologies of specialization, the reduction in the size of a sector will generate spillover damages that will offset the spillover gains generated by the expansion of another sector. In this situation, the propositions outlined are generally valid. Only when the subsectors of the economy differ in their potential for utilization of technologies of specialization will the propositions require modification.

that there is an externality involved in an individual's work-leisure choice and that any participant in an economy has an economic interest in the work supply of others. And I have suggested that individualized adjustments in the work-choice margin that might be dictated by what I have called "naked preferences" will generate overall results that are nonoptimal or inefficient. In such a setting, I have suggested that all could be made better off, on their own account, if everyone agrees to work more.

Let me indicate carefully what I have not claimed here. Strictly speaking, I have not suggested that as of 1992 in the United States workers supply too few hours to the market. Actual working time depends, to an extent, on many institutional factors not taken into account in my discussion, which is exclusively devoted to an examination of the choice margin when work supply is variable. Even within these limits, however, I do not claim that individuals now supply too little or too much work to the market. (In this sense, my title for the chapter is misleading.) The point I seek to make is that an ethic of work—that psychological state which tells us, internally, that work is good and loafing is bad, that makes us feel guilty when we loaf too much—can be interpreted as the means through which we "internalize the work choice externality," to use the terminology of the welfare economist. Somehow or other, in ways that we surely do not understand, a long process of cultural evolution may have embodied in us an ethical norm that does, indeed, benefit us economically. That is to say, we are better off with the work ethic than we should be without it. Our economic well-being is enhanced by the presence of ethical constraints on our behavior that prevent our expedient response to the temptations offered by the examples of the beach boys and the flower children.[2]

Even if my argument is accepted in its entirety, there is no means of ascertaining just how strong the work ethic need be, or how widespread it must be among the work force, to internalize effectively the economic externality. The argument suggests that within some limits, the presence of a work ethic exerts beneficial effects. But it is clearly possible that, in some circumstances, the ethical constraints can become overly severe and act to reduce rather than increase individuals' well-being; perhaps in modern Singapore or Taiwan the work choice margin is extended beyond economically efficient boundaries, as ideally determined by some omniscient observer. My own sense is that in the United States today the strength of the "Puritan" work ethic has been seriously eroded, both directly at the level of individual supplies of labor, as discussed here, and indirectly as evidenced by the apparent willingness to support, through both private and public agencies, those persons who are unproductive as a result of their own choices. I should

[2]Ethical constraints or rules, as means of correcting or internalizing relevant externalities, are, of course, alternatives to possible legal-political constraints. With the work-leisure margin of choice, however, political internalization seems to offer little prospect of success. For further discussion, see Buchanan (1991a); see also Congleton (1991).

think that those persons who are members of generations later than my own feel less guilty when they loaf than members of my generation do, on average, and, further, that members of generations to come will escape still further from the ethical constraint. And we should make no mistake about the consequences; the growth in the productivity of the economy must decline.

VIII. IN CONCLUSION

I have tried to present an argument that would seem convincing both to those who are not familiar with textbook-level economic analysis and to those who, to this extent, classify themselves as economic sophisticates. I suspect that the argument will have been more appealing to the first group than to the second, since ordinary common sense suggests that we do become richer as the size of the market expands. Once this relationship is acknowledged, the economic benefits of a work ethic, which does make us work harder than we would in its absence, become obvious.

The economists among you probably remain skeptical, despite the logical structure of my argument. I have not responded to what may be the economists' major objection to my analysis. Is not leisure a "good" like anything else? Do we not define "goods" subjectively? If we do, why is leisure any different from apples, sealing wax, and compact disc players?

My response is quite straightforward. Leisure is

different from other valued end uses of resources because it is, and must be, a nonmarket good and, hence,
beyond the set of goods that are produced with the
network of economic interdependence that determines
the range of specialization. Each person produces his or
her own leisure; specialization in production of this
good is logically impossible.

   This point will, I hope, be clarified in chapter 2,
where I attempt to extend essentially the same analysis
to the ethic of saving and capital formation, which
offers a second means through which persons may, in
their own choices, act to expand the supply of inputs to
the market nexus.

Chapter 2

We Should All Save More:
The Economics of the Saving Ethic

I. INTRODUCTION

In chapter 1, I argue that the economic well-being of anyone, by his or her own standards, depends on the behavioral attitude toward work held by the rest of us and that we have, to an extent, internalized this particular sort of interdependence through the work ethic. Hence, the subtitle for chapter 1 is "The Economic Value of the Work Ethic." In a literal sense, my argument amounts to an analytical defense of a central element in what is often called loosely "Puritan ethics."

I shall not summarize that argument here, but my central analytical proposition may be briefly restated. Work, the supply of labor input to the market, is a

means through which the size of the production-
exchange nexus, the market itself, may be quantitatively determined. And the supply of more work by
participants in the economy implies a larger economy,
a larger market, which, in turn, implies that the
advantages of division and specialization of labor can
be exploited more fully than in a smaller economy. And
each of us, in our role as user or consumer of final
goods, prefers to live in an economy where more
economic value rather than less is available in exchange
for any given amount of input effort. We want "more
bang for the buck," no matter how many "bucks" we
may have accumulated or how many we may earn.

For those among you who are economic sophisticates, the extension of the argument to saving and
capital formation may be straightforward. But since
even my argument on the effects of the work ethic may
not be wholly accepted, especially by my professional
economist peers, some variation of the analysis in
application to saving may not be out of order here. And
again let us keep in mind the statement made by
Herbert Spencer in the preface to his book *The Data of
Ethics* (n.d.: vii): "Only by varied reiteration can alien
conceptions be forced on reluctant minds."

Also, you will recall that I stated in the introduction
to chapter 1 that the support of the proposition that we
should all save more is both more persuasive in the
sense of public acceptability in currently popular cli-
mates of opinion and more difficult to sustain analytically than the analogous proposition that we should all

work more than we do. That is to say, there are important differences between the supply of work and the supply of saving and in the accompanying ethical norms that may affect individual attitudes toward these margins of choice. My decision to increase the number of hours worked per week is different from my decision to increase the rate of saving out of my current income, both in terms of my own sense of utility or satisfaction and in the ultimate economic effects on others than me. These differences require examination in some detail.

In section II, I review, very briefly, the origins of the widespread public and professional dissatisfaction with current rates of saving in the United States and the accompanying normative agreement that saving rates are too low and should be increased. Those who share this view will be initially prejudiced to accept my argument in this chapter, although the ultimate grounding of the norm may remain quite different from that which I develop here. My own argument grounds the evaluative judgment that savings may be too low on the welfare analytics of individuals' choices rather than on any presumed knowledge of appropriate macroaggregate objectives. I also examine, again briefly, the view that current saving rates are too low but only because of various governmental policies, notably those that involve spending, taxing, and deficit creation, that discriminate against savings, with the implication that if governmental actions could, in fact, be made neutral as between savings and other uses of income, the normative argument in favor of more savings would vanish.

In section III, it is necessary to place the whole argument in an appropriately qualified macroeconomic setting. Many of us remain partially trapped in the Keynesian-inspired delusion that fails to make the proper separation between monetary-macro institutional structures and the choices between current and future uses of income. It is this set of Keynesian ideas that is at least partially responsible for the change in attitudes toward saving that has been descriptive of the middle and last decades of this century.

In section IV, I distinguish categorically between the argument that I advance here and that which introduces a normative or evaluative judgment concerning our generalized obligations, or lack thereof, to future generations of persons, to posterity, as it were. The whole set of issues raised under the rubric of our obligations to the future is both important and intellectually fascinating. But intergenerational ethics is not my subject matter. My argument is advanced in support of the proposition that we should all save more, not for our childrens' or our grandchildrens' sake at all but in our own multiperiod economic interest. We may, essentially, finesse intergenerational ethics issues altogether by postulating that the analysis applies to persons with multiperiod time horizons.

Sections II, III, and IV are all preliminary to the central argument, which is explicitly introduced only in section V. By necessity, the first step in the analysis involves definitional clarification. Just what is saving? And what presuppositions of the analytical models are required to equate an increase in saving with an increase in the size of the market nexus? An elementary, and I hope limited, excursus into the intricacies of capital theory is dictated. Section VI introduces a summary comparison of the effects of increases in savings and increases in work effort. Section VII examines the internalization of the externality involved in saving choices through ethical constraints. Section VIII looks at alternative means for correction and concludes the chapter.

II. HOW MUCH "SHOULD" BE SAVED?

Much of the current policy discussion about the low rate of aggregate savings in the United States seems to accept, with little critical examination, the notion that there are ways of determining how much we should save, in the aggregate. And, by inference, economists-experts can tell us whether current practice meets the exogenously settled standard. Note that in my argument of this chapter, I do not need to be able to say just how much "should" be saved, in the aggregate, despite the proposition that we "should" save more than we do. My stance in this respect will seem paradoxical only to those who do not understand or who do not appreciate the individualistic evaluative framework that I try consistently to adopt. I can suggest that individuals, acting strictly in their own interest, should save more than they do when each person acts as if there is no interdependency among the separate saving choices made by separate persons. I can advance this argument while at the same time refusing to be drawn into a position that involves evoking some external criterion for deciding what an optimal rate of saving might be. My own methodological paradigm will, perhaps, be more fully evident as the analysis proceeds. For now, I want to examine briefly the claims advanced by those who are quite willing to adjudge the savings rate that exists to be lower than some ideal standard that must, presumably, offer the objective for policy.

By almost any measure, aggregate savings in the United States in the 1990s are relatively low, both by comparison with savings in other developed countries and with savings in earlier periods of our history. Dispute continuously rages among quantitatively inclined economists and econometricians concerning the appropriate procedures for measuring what it is desired to measure when rates of saving are discussed. What items should and should not be included? I do not have either the competence or the interest to take part in such disputes, even indirectly and at second hand.

With reference to the international league tables, and no matter how we measure what it is that we measure, the rate of savings out of current income in the United States falls well below that of other developed countries. Net national savings as a share of total product lies somewhere within the range of between

2 ½ and 5 percent, whereas in Japan this ratio is three to four times as large, roughly in the range of 15 to 18 percent. Developed countries in Europe exhibit aggregate savings rates that fall between these limits. And, historically, the savings rate in the United States has been falling through recent years, except for a possible reversal only in the early 1990s.

Those who evaluate the macroeconomic performance of whole "national economies" are influenced both by the international comparisons and by the historical record. Economies that exhibit low rates of saving do not grow rapidly, and rates of growth, as measured, are widely accepted to be appropriate criteria for national success or failure. But who is to specify whether the savings rate in the United States is "too low" or the savings rate in Japan is "too high"? Some of the confusion on this point is exemplified in the amusing suggestions of American politicians to the effect that the Japanese should be required to relax and go on spending sprees. Stripped to its essentials, the criticism of U.S. savings habits based on vague macroeconomic performance criteria does not seem convincing, despite its widespread popularity.

A somewhat more defensible position is that which adjudges the aggregate savings rate to be too low but only because of governmental policies that discriminate against the savings behavior of individuals and institutions. The inference is that aggregate savings would increase, perhaps substantially, if politics did not intervene in the workings of the economy.

This charge is clearly on target to the extent that the net dissaving of the federal government, in the form of its large and persistent budgetary deficits, does, indeed, make up a substantial negative item in the accounts. This item, alone, goes far toward explaining the shortfall in current savings rates below historical trends in the United States. If, as if by some magic, the budget deficit could be eliminated, the net savings rate would be substantially higher than it now is. Much the same inference would be drawn, at least by some observers, with reference to the discrimination against savings choices that describes the tax structure, at all levels of government in the United States. By contrast and as pointed out by still other observers, there are features of the legal-institutional environment in the United States that may differentially favor savings and capital formation, as witness limited liability for corporate investment and relatively favorable treatment of intergenerational transfers of wealth.

In any case, it is not necessary that I examine in detail either of the familiar arguments for policy measures designed to increase the aggregate rate of saving. I have noted the existence of such arguments in this section solely for the purpose of suggesting that my central proposition to the effect that we should save more may find acceptance based on reasons that are quite different from those that I shall advance. In this respect, the choice to save more is quite different, in both public and professional perception, from the choice to work more.

III. THE GREAT KEYNESIAN DELUSION

I shall now digress from the main line of discussion to forestall possible confusion and misunderstanding that may arise in interpreting my argument. This misunderstanding may stem from what I shall here call "the great Keynesian delusion," which exerted a significant influence on public, scientific, and political attitudes during several decades of this century. I refer to the Keynesian delusion, because it was Lord Keynes who offered the intellectual-analytical formulation of the proposition that exerted such major effects on the thinking of economists and policymakers and that continues to affect attitudes toward saving behavior even in this last decade of the century.

The central Keynesian proposition was often presented, particularly in elementary economics textbooks, as "the paradox of thrift" or "the paradox of saving." The argument suggested that efforts of income earners to save more, to save larger shares of current income, might backfire and that, in the net, aggregate savings might fall if too many persons tried to save, due to the feedbacks on the flow of incomes. The so-called fallacy of composition was introduced to explain why individualized choices, separately made, might generate results that may be contrary to those desired by all persons in the nexus.

To get some sense of the appeal of the Keynesian proposition here, it is useful to recall the economic-political-institutional environment during the time that the proposition was first articulated. The 1930s were the years of the Great Depression. Almost one-fourth of the American labor force was unemployed during the worst of those years, and the problem was widely interpreted to be a breakdown of the market or capitalist economy and, more specifically, as a failure of this economy to generate a demand for its production sufficiently large to take potential supplies off the market. That is to say, the diagnosis was one that attributed failure to *underconsumption*. Hence the remedy was to be found in spending, whether private or public.

In this model, the act of saving, which represents a withdrawal from the circular flow of income or an abstinence from spending, exerts negative or undesired effects at the macroeconomic level. Business spending on plant, equipment, inventories, and labor is directly responsive to observed rates of spending on goods and services by individuals, firms, and governments. The Keynesian diagnosis was that saving was excessive rather than deficient, and public policies were advocated which would expand rates of spending. Public opinion was urged to shift toward generalized praise for expressed willingness to spend.

This diagnosis and the subsequent prescription for the macroeconomic illness of the Great Depression were characterized by a tragic failure to recognize the importance of the political-institutional framework, both in providing the environmental setting appropriate for satisfactory macroeconomic performance and in offering corrective offsets to changes in individual pro-

pensities to hoard. In the early 1930s the aggregate rate
of spending was, indeed, depressed, and desperate measures were needed to increase that rate. But the fundamental source of the trouble was wrongly identified in
the Keynesian analysis. The source was squarely located
in the failure of the monetary authority, the Federal
Reserve System, which allowed the supply of money to
fall dramatically as the banking-financial crisis deep-
ened; whereas, as we now know, the proper action should
have been just the opposite. We now know that almost
any policy action would have dictated that the monetary
authority maintain stability or even growth in the monetary aggregates. And had this result been ensured, there
would have been no Great Depression, as such. The
macroeconomy of the United States would have absorbed
any temporary shock, including that which originated in
the banking structure, and the jerry-built Keynesian
analysis, which ignored institutional failures, need not
have emerged at all.

And, important for my purpose here, individual participants in the economy need not have been misled into
an acceptance of attitudes that attribute to consumption
spending some praiseworthy social status while placing a
social stigma of sorts on saving. The whole set of problems that involves monetary-macroeconomic-institu-
tional performance, along with the criteria for success
and failure, need not have become mixed up and confused
with individuals' choices to spend or to save.

I need not, of course, use this occasion to defend my
own analysis and interpretation of either the Great

Depression or my criticism of the confusion in the intellectual-analytical responses. I have included this summary section only for the purpose of averting possible misunderstanding of my enterprise. When I suggest that we should save more and that we should do so in our own general interest, I am assuming that the institutional framework is such as to allow the effects of private choices to be separated from conditions of macroeconomic stability.

IV. OBLIGATIONS TO FUTURE GENERATIONS

I need to clear away one more set of extraneous notions before getting to the meat of this chapter's theme. To the extent that is possible, I need to divorce my argument from apparently related normative principles that invoke considerations of intergenerational ethics, principles that ground saving norms in intergenerational justice, that defend saving behavior and propositions to increase savings in terms of obligations to those who live in periods of time after that in which savings decisions are made, that is, future generations. I consider the whole range of questions that concern our obligations to the future, privately or collectively, to be of great importance, and I do not think that moral-ethical philosophers (and economists) have devoted enough attention to such questions. The difficulty of getting analytical handles on the problems involved should not be allowed to inhibit intellectual effort.

Within the limits of my enterprise, however, I do not need to resort to the treatment of future generations as a justification for my argument in support of increasing rates of personal saving beyond those that emerge from the independent choices of persons. To the extent that such intergenerational arguments can be adduced to supplement and support those that I advance, in particular, if such arguments serve to bolster the force of a saving ethic, they become welcome additions to practical efforts to implement my analysis. But the normative distinction between the two sets of arguments must be kept clearly in mind. Arguments that suggest we should save more because we have obligations to future generations that are not fully reflected in current choices to save necessarily introduce interpersonal and intergenerational comparisons of utilities, comparisons that my argument avoids, as later discussion will indicate.

Consider an individual who makes an independent and wholly voluntary choice to save, say, five dollars out of each one hundred dollars of income earned. In the standard theory of choice, we should say that at the margin between spending and saving, this person secures an anticipated utility from a dollar's worth of saving that is equal to that anticipated from a dollar's worth of spending. To say that such a person should save more because, by so doing, the utility of those who may come along later, the children or grandchildren, whether of the individual

who saves or of others, will be increased is to presume, somehow, that the interests of these future
period members are not accurately taken into account in current savings choices. But who is to
judge, and on what criteria? How are the utilities of
those in future periods to be measured and put up
against the utilities of the individual who makes the
current period choices?

A crude utilitarian calculus may even be adduced to
suggest that rather than saving more, persons who are
now living should actually save less. If the economy is
expected to continue to grow through time, for exogenous reasons, income levels per person promise to be
higher in future periods than those levels now observed. Hence, naive utilitarianism might suggest
that, on simple egalitarian or redistributive norms,
persons now living should, to the extent possible,
receive transfers from those who will live later, rather
than the reverse. Some downward adjustment in freely
chosen rates of savings might thus be contemplated,
including the dissaving represented by the government's budget deficits.

This last argument may seem bizarre, but I introduce it here only to indicate that any effort to justify
increased rates of saving out of current income because
of concern for future generations may backfire. Intergenerational ethics should concern us. But if we can
construct an argument for more savings without resort
to intergenerational comparisons, we remain that much
ahead of a very complex game.

V. SAVING, CAPITAL,
AND THE EXTENT OF THE MARKET

I am now at the point where I can begin to develop my
central proposition. But first let me summarize what I
have already said here. I have disengaged the discussion from the macroeconomic policy debates about the
alleged low rates of saving; I have warned against
mixing the savings choices made by individuals and
the overall performance characteristics of macromonetary institutions; and I have suggested that concerns
about obligations to future generations are irrelevant
to my argument.

What, then, is my argument all about? In one sense,
the proposition is very simple; but in another sense, it
is quite complex. Simply put, the proposition states
that the act of saving allows for a release of resources
into the production of capital rather than consumer
goods and that this increase in capital inputs into the
market operates in essentially the same fashion as an
increase in the supply of labor inputs (as discussed in
chap. 1). The increase in capital expands the size of the
economy, and this, in turn, allows for an increased
exploitation of the division and specialization of resources. The economic value of output per unit of input
expands, and this result ensures that all persons in the
economic nexus, whether workers, savers, or consum-
ers, are made better off and on their own terms.

This summary statement of the proposition is accurate, but it does slide by several subsidiary steps in the

analysis that must be clarified. When considered at an individual level, just what is involved in an act of saving? To save is not to spend. The flow of income received by an individual allows for voluntary disposition into two composite categories: (1) spending on purchases of final or end items of consumption and (2) saving. In a real sense, savings are a residual; they measure the amount of income left over after spending on goods and services. But what form does this savings take? The individual does not simply withdraw purchasing power from the circular income flow of the economy. The funds saved are allowed to return to the circular flow by being made available to those persons and institutions who utilize them to purchase *capital goods*.

(In the simplest model, we could think of the same person acting in both the saving and the investing roles here. Robinson Crusoe saves by forgoing the gathering of coconuts long enough to build the fishing net, a capital good. As we know, however, much of the whole Keynesian analysis was based on the recognition that the act of saving is not equivalent to the act of investment and that different persons may play different roles. It seems best, therefore, to think initially in terms of the institutional arrangements that allow funds saved by an individual to become available to those who actually carry out the purchases of capital goods separately. If the macromonetary framework is in place, and if these institutions function properly, an act of saving will find its accompaniment in an act of capital goods purchase. A dollar of new saving, a dollar not spent on purchasing final goods and services, allows for a dollar's purchase of capital goods.)

As a first pass, there might seem to be no effect on the inclusive size of the economic nexus in a switch from the purchase of a consumption good to the purchase of a capital good. There would, of course, be a change in the composition of production as the allocation of resources responds to the shift in demands. If persons increase their rates of saving from current income, with offsetting reductions in consumption spending, the economy responds by generating expanded quantities of capital goods and reduced quantities of consumption goods. The aggregate size of the production-exchange nexus would not seem to be modified in the process. The shift to more savings does not seem, at a first pass, to be at all analogous to the shift from nonwork to work, which does, directly, expand the size of the economic or market nexus at the expense of the nonmarket sector.

This account, however, overlooks a fundamental feature of economic life, the productivity of capital. If that which is purchased as a result of the release of funds from the outlay on consumption goods and services should be nothing more than storable quantities of the latter, there would be no net increase in the size of the economy as a result of the behavioral change. But capital goods are not properly modeled as consumption goods in stored form. Capital goods are instruments, or tools, that are used ultimately in the production of final goods. Capital goods are inputs to the production processes.

The essential characteristic of capital, as an abstract notion, is that it is productive. The precise meaning of the word "productive" in the sense used here must be clarified, especially since the application to capital goods has been the source of much confusion in the history of economic ideas. Loosely speaking, any input that is transformed into valued output is productive; the input is employed to valued purpose. But this general usage is not what is meant by the term "productive" in the sense required for the analysis here. To say that capital is productive is to say that the value produced by the employment of capital is greater than the value that is given up or sacrificed in the production or acquisition of capital. That is to say, capital goods produce a surplus, over and beyond their cost of production. This productive surplus is, however, generated only in time. (The immediate transformation of a purchased capital good into current consumption goods would not, of course, yield any surplus at all.) This productivity through time, and only through time, has caused many economists to attribute the net productivity to time itself rather than to the attributes of capital, with undue intellectual confusion in the process. The elementary fact is that if used through time, capital goods yield a surplus over and above the return required to amortize fully the initial value of outlay. The investment of a dollar today yields a productive return of, say, 5 percent over a year's time, for a gross return of $1.05.

This simple numerical example makes my point. The economy, one year hence, is larger by five cents than the economy today when the decision is made to save and to invest the additional dollar, to withdraw this dollar from the spending on consumption goods. And when the economy next year increases in size, there can be increased prospects for specialization in resource use, with the resultant effects traced in chapter 1.

It may, nonetheless, be useful to trace these effects in specific application to savings choices. Return to the numerical example above. The person who chooses to save the extra dollar today does so in the full expectation that he or she will receive $1.05 a year from today. One motivation for the saving in the first place is surely the knowledge of the opportunity to secure a larger value in the future than the value that must be given up today, as measured in the sacrifice currently of consumption goods and services. But how do others in the economy get any benefit from the saving decision of that person who does, today, withdraw the additional dollar from the stream of consumption spending? In terms of the example, it would seem that the person who saves, and this person alone, gets the full return on the investment that the saving makes possible, the full surplus generated by the productivity of capital over time. The 5 percent return over the initial outlay is owed to and paid to the person who sets aside the dollar, who abstains from consuming in exchange for the opportunity to increase his or her income next year.

As with the work supply externality, however, there exist spillover benefits from the saving decision. As noted, the economy, as measured by the total value of product, becomes larger by the size of the increment to value reflected in the net product of the capital investment that the initial act of saving makes possible. To be sure, the additional sources available for spending, on both consumer and capital goods, in the second year must come from the person who first saves and later receives this net return. But this person, in the second year, is able to return to the consumption spending or the capital spending stream, or both, $1.05, which becomes the demand for goods and services produced in the economy. And an economy that is larger, if even by five cents, is able to exploit more fully the advantages of specialization in resource usage. Put the one additional savings dollar together with others that reflect like decisions on the part of many persons, and a technology somewhere that was just on the margin of economic viability may be pushed beyond the threshold of survivability.

The analysis is on all fours with that outlined in chapter 1 in which I discussed the supply of additional labor, in the form of more work. Individual participants in an economy, through their own choices of work-versus-leisure in the one case and spending-versus-saving in the other, can increase their own economic well-being by acting in such fashion as to incorporate in their own behavior the interdependencies among their separately made choices in supplying both labor and saving inputs to the market.

VI. A DOLLAR SAVED IS A DOLLAR EARNED: A QUANTITATIVE COMPARISON

A dollar's saving represents an initial withdrawal from the consumption spending stream, which makes possible a dollar's addition to the demand for and purchase of capital goods. The increase in the measured size of the economy occurs only because capital is productive. In the next period, the economy is larger by the amount of the net product of capital, that is, the return over and above full depreciation. This simple analysis seems to suggest that a new dollar of savings is much less effective in generating an increase in the size of the economy than a new dollar earned as a result of an expansion in the quantity of hours worked. The latter expands the size of the production-exchange nexus by a full dollar's worth, whereas a new dollar of savings expands the nexus in the next period by only, say, five cents.

The simple analysis in this respect is quite misleading, however, because it overlooks the fact that capital, once created, is *permanent*, in terms of its economic value. A dollar of new savings, today, makes possible an increase in investment in productive capital that will yield a return over and above full depreciation, not only in the first period after the initial increment to saving-investment but in all future periods. Hence, the present discounted value of the increase in the size of the economic nexus that is generated by a new dollar of savings is a dollar (assuming that the investment yields the average rate of return and that this rate of return is also the rate of interest at which yields are discounted). In present-value terms, therefore, the dollar of new savings is quantitatively the same in effect as the dollar of new earnings from an increase in work supplied to the market.

Nonetheless, the timing of the market's expansion remains different in the two cases. The once-and-for-all increase in the supply of work may stimulate an immediate introduction of new technology made viable by the earnings increase in effective size. The present-value increase in the economy's effective size consequent on an increment in capital formation made possible by new saving may stimulate a somewhat slower rate of sustainable technological advance.

VII. INTERNALIZATION THROUGH AN ETHIC OF SAVING

In both chapters 1 and 2, my enterprise is primarily positive in the scientific meaning of this term, despite the deliberately assertive statements used for the chapters' main titles. The two subtitles are descriptively more accurate. My purpose is to demonstrate that both an ethic of work and an ethic of saving, basic components of that set of attitudes often summarized under the rubric "Puritan ethics," retain positive economic content, even in the last decade of the twentieth century. That is to say, to the extent that these ethical constraints exist and continue to influence individual choice behavior, we are better off than we should be in their total absence. And in this summary statement, as elsewhere, I use the term "better off" strictly with reference to individuals' own evaluations rather than my own or any other set of standards.

In the parlance of modern (Paretian) welfare economics, we *internalize* the externality or the interdependency among our separated decisions to work and to save through the presence in our psyche of a set of ethical constraints that dictate both that we work harder and that we save more than our naked preferences might indicate to us. The strengths of these ethical constraints, hence the degree to which they actually influence choice behavior, will, of course, vary from one person to another, among differing social environments, and also will not remain constant over time. I have suggested in chapter 1 that I sense some erosion in the strength of the work ethic, with predictable consequences.

In this respect, my concern with an erosion of the saving ethic is even more acute. Among large numbers of the American labor force, despite some erosion, a work ethic remains strong. But the observed decline in the aggregate rate of net national savings in the United States cannot be denied to exist. And, once again, the consequences for our own well-being should be clear.

We must become relatively poorer, in our own terms, as we save less, as our economy fails to grow as fast as higher rates of saving might make possible. And this verdict applies to everyone in the economy, quite independent of where a person is located in the intergenerational chain described by positive, and negative, bequests.

It is relatively easy to identify several sources of erosion in the strength of the saving ethic. I have already discussed briefly the Keynesian interpretation of the events of the 1930s, a diagnosis that elevated the "paradox of thrift" to center stage in the attention of economists and that surely, with some time lag, influenced the behavior of politicians in their institutional treatment of incentives. In addition, the social stigma attached to saving behavior has presumably exerted some effect, however slight, on personal spending habits. Financial innovations that have made it easier to spend, especially from income not yet earned, have allowed persons to dissave more readily, thereby making positive saving work harder in offsetting negative entries on national balance sheets.

A somewhat related, but largely independent, development has modified the structure of savings incentives, quite apart from any direct operation of ethical constraints. I refer to the emergence of the welfare-transfer state during the course of this century. A shorthand description might classify this development as the politicization or collectivization of that element in saving that had previously been motivated both by life cycle and intergenerational bequest consideration. Politicized schemes for social insurance against income loss during retirement years are the institutional embodiments of these changes. As experience suggests, governments have proved willing to issue promises to ensure retirement income support, but they have generally been unwilling to levy taxes for the purpose of accumulating earning assets sufficient to cover future period costs. In effect, the social security system, the system for meeting retirement income needs, has been financed from current income flows rather than from productive capital investment.

As a participant in the politicized system, the individual is motivated to reduce those savings that might have otherwise been set aside to secure income flows during retirement years. This result need not accompany politicization of a retirement or pension scheme. But such a neutral effect on aggregate savings would be produced only if the collectivized scheme is, itself, maintained on some actuarially sound basis. The failure of democratically elected legislatures to take steps to accumulate fund balances sufficient to meet pension obligations has been characteristic of the American system, since its inception in the 1930s.

In a more general sense and beyond any politicization of what might be called the organization of individualized accounts, the dramatic increase in the transfer sector of the economy has undermined incentives to save and to invest. To the extent that persons are led to expect that governmental transfer payments

will be available to them as members of this or that
group who qualify for eligibility as a consequence of
this or that event or circumstance, their planning
against many contingencies need not occur. And, of
course, the taxes that are levied to finance such transfers make any such saving from income more difficult.
The "cradle to grave" security promised in the idealized slogan of the welfare-transfer state stands as an
open invitation to the individual to live hand to
mouth, almost as a direct complement to the politicization of transfers.

Superimposed on the emergence of the welfare-
transfer state in this century was the experience of
inflation, especially during the decade of the 1970s in
the United States. Even for those persons who desire to
carry out individualized savings plans for life cycle,
bequest, or other motives, inflationary expectations
make real saving difficult. Monetary instruments carry
no assurance of maintenance of real value through
time, and precepts of rational choice behavior dictate
shifts of demand to real goods, with a clear bias toward
items of consumption, current or durable. And consumer durables, although they yield benefits over
time, do not qualify as productive capital in the
analysis sketched out earlier.

The family, as a cohesive unit that extends beyond
the lives of its individual members and that becomes
the institutional base for intergenerational transmission of accumulated wealth (capital value), has
become less important in our whole scheme of social

interaction. Even the limited ethical constraint that sometimes instructed members of wealthy families not to "eat up the capital" has lost much of its influence.

The listing of causes for shifts in behavior toward consumption spending and away from saving could be extended. But the analysis here is limited largely to a partial explanation of the effects of the shifts rather than the causes.

VIII. ALTERNATIVES TO RESTORATION OF A SAVING ETHIC

In the United States of 1993, it is probably not fully rational for the individual, or the family unit, to save more than a somewhat limited share of income, a share sufficient to meet personal contingencies that do not, as yet, qualify for subsidization under welfare-transfer programs. If residues of an old-fashioned, Puritan-style ethic cause persons to save more than the objective elements in their individualized choice settings dictate to be rational in some strict sense, we are all benefited by way of the external effects outlined earlier. But it should be clear that the force of any such ethical norm must continue to erode further in the face of continuing, and possibly still accelerating, shifts in incentive structures. "The state will take care of you" — this is the hymnal of modernity. Why should we expect, from ethics or any other source, individuals to save much at all?

The interesting feature of the political environment of the 1990s is that there seems to be a developing recognition of the effects of the low savings rate on economic growth and also an acknowledgment that the incentive structure of the tax-transfer system (along with the budget deficit) is a relevant causal factor. It is not out of the range of plausible prediction to suggest that sometime during the 1990s we may observe attempts at *political internalization* of the interdependencies among individual savings choices. This political alternative to ethical correction could not be predicted with respect to the work supply externality. Hence, in this respect at least, an ethic of work continues to be more important than an ethic of saving. But, in one sense, political action aimed at restoration of incentives to save and invest, although not taking the form of imposing ethical constraints on individual choice at all, may reflect at least an indirect recognition of the economic interdependencies stressed in this chapter.

Another way of making this same point is to say that the whole nest of concerns about the low rates of aggregate savings, by international or historical standards of comparison, that seem to be grounded in criteria of macroeconomic performance, such as measured rates of growth, may ultimately be grounded in some implicit and inarticulated acceptance of the analysis that I have outlined here. Or, as perhaps is more likely, we may get political action designed to increase rates of saving for reasons that are unrelated to the arguments here advanced, reasons that may be based on questionable analytical foundations, whether positive or normative. Be that as it may, any effective measures to increase savings may, within limits, be analytically grounded on considerations of our own interests, and efforts to elaborate our understanding of the economic interdependencies among our separate savings choices can proceed in tandem with practical steps toward reform in the incentive structures.

Chapter 3

We Should All Pay the Preacher:
Economic Origins of
Ethical Constraints

I. INTRODUCTION

In chapters 1 and 2, I have subjected two of the central principles in what is sometimes referred to as "Puritan ethics" to economic analysis. I think that I have demonstrated that an ethic of work and an ethic of saving have economic value in the sense that each of the participants in an economy benefits from the presence of these ethical attitudes among others with whom the participant expects to interact in a large and complex production-exchange nexus. That is to say, the pres-

---

A more formal version of some parts of the analysis developed in this chapter is presented in my paper, "Economic Origins of Ethical Constraints" (Buchanan 1991*b*).

ence of these ethics, to work and to save, over and beyond those choices that might simply be dictated by naked preferences, is economically functional. They serve a positive economic purpose. I do not want, however, to commit the functionalist fallacy here, represented by an attempt to explain practices, habits, ethics, and institutions by demonstrating that they may be shown to be functional in some societal sense. To explain the presence of the ethic of work or saving, it is necessary to locate origins in the rational choice calculus of individuals at some stage of their development.

There are at least three lines of inquiry that might be taken in a search for economic origins of ethical norms. The first may be described under the rubric "the economics of self-control" or, conversely, "the economics of temptation." The individual, in isolation, may find it advantageous, in his or her long-term interest, to impose binding constraints on his or her own behavior, quite apart from the actions of others. The second program might qualify under the term "constitutional" or "contractarian"; the individual may find it rational to agree to the adoption of conventions or norms that will constrain his or her own action *in exchange* for like constraints on the actions of others. I discuss these two approaches briefly in section II, largely for the purpose of suggesting that these will not be the focus of emphasis in this exercise. I shall concentrate on a third line of inquiry, to be developed more fully in section III. In the analysis here, the economic origins of ethical norms are sought not in the individual's choice of constraints that are aimed to inhibit his or her own behavior, either in isolation or as part of a contractual convention, but instead in the individual's desire for constraints on the behavior of others. In this program, it is necessary to examine carefully what the individual would most prefer that others do in their interactions. "How do I want others to behave, both in general and toward me in particular?" This question, rather than "How do I want to behave?" becomes the starting point for ethical norms or precepts. And note that it is with respect to the behavior of others that preaching may become privately productive for me. Hence, the basis emerges for the assertion in the main title to this chapter.

Section IV outlines the presuppositions that must be accepted for the question to be posed at all, at least by economists who remain roughly within their disciplinary boundaries. Section V offers a rough-and-ready classification of familiar ethical norms in accordance with the criterion suggested by the question. Section VI examines investment in ethical persuasion, including a treatment of the publicness elements in preaching. Section VII relates the discussion to Weber's controversial thesis concerning the possible Puritan (notably Calvinistic) sources of the spirit of capitalism. Section VIII concludes the chapter by summarizing Part I of the book as a unit.

II. SELF-IMPOSED MORAL CONSTRAINTS, SINGLY OR IN CONCERT WITH OTHERS

We may start from the premise that individual behavior is morally-ethically constrained. We do not behave opportunistically in each and every encounter; we do not act in accordance with some "as-if" cost-benefit reckoning, as might be made against the formal legal structure of rewards and penalties. Many of us do not steal, even if we should be certain that there is no possibility of discovery, apprehension, and punishment.

For some purposes, it may suffice to recognize that the moral constraints that guide some aspects of our behavior have evolved in the long process of cultural evolution and that we cannot expect to understand either their origins or their internal logic. At best we can appreciate their functional value. This position is best exemplified in the later work of F. A. Hayek (1979). More ambitious efforts may be directed at explaining the origins of at least some of the ethical norms that may be empirically observed. As noted in the introduction, my primary focus is on the individual's evaluation of constraints on others than himself or herself. But before entering into a discussion of this main argument, it will be helpful to look briefly at self-imposed constraints, either those chosen by the individual in isolation or those chosen in concert with others in some contractlike exchange of behavioral limits.

The logo of the new journal, *Constitutional Political Economy*,[1] is a line drawing of Ulysses bound tightly to the mast as his ship sails past the sirens' shore. He has instructed his oarsmen to bind him and to ignore his entreaties for release. At the commencement of the voyage, Ulysses chose, deliberately, to constrain his own behavior in the predicted future period setting. The selection of the constraint was a part of a fully rational calculus, during which an individualistic constitution was put in place. The constraint was designed as a means of preventing the expedient response to temptation, to short-run or local advantage, that was predicted to be adjudged erroneous and damaging to long-term interests.[2]

Generally, we tend to impose constraints on our own choice behavior when we do not trust our own situational responses to the choice options that may confront us subsequently. This absence of trust in our ability to choose may, as in the case of Ulysses, find its source in our acknowledged weakness of will, our predicted proclivity to act expediently against our own long-term interests. Or, somewhat differently, the lack of trust may arise from our prediction that we will simply be unable to respond correctly to some of the choice options we may face. We may not know how to respond carefully, and we may not recognize the impli-

---

[1]Published by the Center for Study of Public Choice, George Mason University, under the editorship of Professors Viktor Vanberg and Richard Wagner.

[2]For a more technical treatment, see David Levy (1988).

cations of the choice alternatives. These cognitive limits of our capacities, especially in situations that are unfamiliar to us, may make it rational to adopt relatively rigid rules or constraints, some of which may be moral in nature.[3]

Economists are perhaps more comfortable with models in which persons impose constraints on their own behavior but only in a contractual exchange process. The limits on one's own liberty to act expediently in response to any situation that may arise is accepted as a part of a bargain with others whose actions are similarly constrained. These models provide the logical structure for the derivation of constitutional rules from the rational choices of individuals. And the research program developed from such models has, properly, concentrated on political and legal constraints on human action, whether private or public.[4]

There is, however, no analytical basis for restricting contractarian explanation to political and legal rules. Although they must necessarily be less formal, ethical rules may also find some part of their explanation and force in the implicit contractual process that describes the ongoing operation of a moral community of indi-

---

[3]The argument here is based on the work of my colleague, Ron Heiner, who has extended the analysis to explain the emergence of instinctual behavior patterns in many species over the whole period of evolutionary development. See Ron Heiner (1983).

[4]For an early discussion applicable to public constraints, see James M. Buchanan and Gordon Tullock (1962). For an attempt to derive a contractarian logic of private constraints, see David Gauthier (1985).

viduals. In such a setting, the individual participant
need not impose constraints on his or her own behavior
in any isolated calculus of long-term benefit. Instead,
constraints are accepted as the "price" that must be
paid, the "bad" that must be suffered, to secure the
expected "good" that is represented by the reciprocal
constraints on their behavior that others accept as their
part of the contractual exchange.

III. THE INDIVIDUAL'S INTEREST
IN OTHERS' BEHAVIOR

In one sense, the economist, qua economist, can never
get beyond the contractual model of interaction, and
any argument to the effect that ethical norms have
economic content must ultimately resort to the contractarian's evaluative standard. Hence, in the earlier
chapters, when I argued that the work and saving
ethics affect our well-being, in our own terms, I
implicitly invoked the Wicksell-Pareto criterion of
welfare economics, which allows us to work out schemes
through which all participants in the economy can be
brought into agreement. In any contractual exchange
process, whether potential trade is between two parties
or among a large number, the economist hones in on
the mutuality of potential gain and on the "price" that
one party must pay to secure that which he or she wants
from the other(s). The whole exercise is grounded on
the recognition that, indeed, each party seeks to
modify the behavior of the other but also on the

supposition that such a behavioral change can be secured only on payment of some price.

Think of a very simple illustration. You have an apple, and I have a quarter. I want you to give me the apple. I seek to modify your behavior in this respect. On the other side, you want me to give you the quarter, hence, to change my behavior. Both of us may gain utility in the potential exchange, but this mutuality of gain should not obscure the initial interdependence. And note that my ideal or bliss situation is not that which is attained by paying you the quarter and getting the apple in return. Instead, my ideal situation is attained only if you *give* me the apple, literally, and I keep the quarter. If I could, somehow, program you to give me an apple when we meet, I get benefits higher than those enjoyed when I am required to pay a price.

I have, therefore, an economic interest in affecting your behavior in such fashion as to yield me extra-exchange benefits. And if you should give me the apple without exacting reciprocal payment, you must be constrained by some internal ethical norm. You are forgoing the opportunity to get the quarter, which you could use, because you are constrained ethically from exacting such payment from me. Clearly, it is in my interest to instill in your psyche ethical constraints of this sort, and I am willing to invest resources to secure these results. Such investment must, of course, be less than the full quarter, since I know that I can get you to give up the apple for this amount. But, clearly, if, say, through an investment of ten cents in your psyche, I can persuade you to give me the apple without entering into the direct exchange, I have improved my position by fifteen cents.

If we look at social interaction in this way, we get a different interpretation of the origins of ethical constraints. Such constraints do not emerge from a rational choice calculus on the part of the person whose behavior is constrained, as is the case with both the self-control and the contractarian models sketched out above, but, instead, from the rational choice calculus of others with whom the person to be constrained is expected to interact in the social nexus. In a sense, this model that locates the origins of ethical constraints in the rationally self-interested calculus of others than the acting individual is both simpler and more strictly "economic" than either of the alternatives.

The model incorporates what we might label as the standard ethical stance for the individual actor who expects to be confronted with choice situations involving other persons. The potential actor-chooser would prefer that he or she retain the option of choosing opportunistically while other partners in the interaction are somehow programmed to behave both predictably and nonopportunistically and in such fashion as to benefit the actor.[5]

Let me return to the simple illustration in which the status quo is described by my possession of a quarter

---

[5]For an early paper that had the same structure of argument, see Buchanan (1965).

and your possession of an apple. My generalized rank-
ing of the alternatives would be as follows:

1) You give me the apple, and I retain the option of
   whether or not to give you the quarter. Your action
   remains independent of my response.
2) You give me the apple, but only if I give you the quarter
   in exchange. Your action is strictly dependent on my
   response.
3) You keep the apple, and I keep the quarter. This is the
   status quo position.
4) I give you the quarter, and you retain the option of
   giving me or not giving me the apple in response. My
   behavior is independent of your response.

The economist has no trouble accepting such an ordering as part of a structure for rational choice. The
economist would go further and suggest that, for you,
the ordering should reverse 1 and 4. And, of course, the
economist concentrates almost exclusive attention on
the superiority of the exchange or trading alternative
over the status quo, for both parties. The economist
ignores, almost totally, the interest that each party
retains in the behavior of the other, outside of and
beyond the comparison between the pretrade and the
posttrade positions.

As a mental experiment, however, let us suppose
that trade or exchange does not exist; this institution
has not yet been invented. The explicit trading option
(2 above) is simply not available to the actors in the
setting as described. In this case, note that in the

rankings as outlined, no alternative that can be institutionally implemented is preferred to the status quo, for
both parties, despite the fact that there does exist a
final position that is mutually preferred. In this setting it is clear that if, somehow, each of the two parties
could, by investment in mutual persuasion, change the
ordering of the other, so that you would genuinely
prefer to give me the apple independent of my response
(1 above) and, at the same time, I should come genuinely to prefer to give you the quarter (4 above)
independent of your response, we could attain the
position described as the result of explicit exchange (2
above), which we both prefer to the status quo but
without resort to the explicit interdependence that
trading reciprocity represents.

How might this mutually beneficial outcome be
achieved under the circumstances here assumed? If preference orderings are amenable to change at all (more on
this in sec. IV), each party will find it advantageous to
invest resources in modifying the preferences of others so
as to produce the desired behavioral changes. If the
institutions of moral-ethical persuasion, which I have
called "the preacher" in the title for this chapter, are even
marginally effective, each party to a potential interaction
will have some incentive to "pay the preacher," that is, to
invest in bringing the orderings of others around to the
directions that will generate the spillover or external
benefits promised.

This simple illustration is also designed for a sec-
ondary purpose, which is that of showing that ex-

change or trade does mitigate and/or minimize the necessary role for ethical constraints in facilitating the achievement of mutually desired outcomes of social interaction. As the illustration indicates, when exchange is not possible, individual behavior that embodies ethical constraints may be required to generate mutually desired results. And, contrariwise, when trade is possible, individuals may not be nearly so concerned about the preference orderings of others in the social nexus. And it is appropriate for the economist to concentrate on the trading process and on institutional design that opens up further opportunities for trade. As D. H. Robertson (1956) once stated, the role of the economist is to issue warning barks whenever he sees proposals advanced which depend on love for their efficacious operation.

By contrast, neither the economist nor anyone else should neglect or ignore the potential economic usefulness of ethical norms, especially in settings where explicit exchange arrangements cannot readily and practicably be implemented. Of particular relevance here are those interactions that involve the simultaneous interdependence among large numbers of participants, where any possible exchange, contract, or trading scheme would be highly complex and difficult to enforce. For such cases, it is "as if" explicit trade is simply not available as a choice option for the participants. And for such cases, the simple illustration without the trade-exchange alternative included can be suggestive.

In this context, think of the specific ethical norms discussed in the first two chapters: the work ethic and the saving ethic. As the analyses showed, all other participants in the inclusively defined production-exchange network, in "the economy," secure benefits from an extension in the work or saving effort of any participant, beyond that amount which would be individually chosen in some parametric adjustment to the objective situation confronted. That is to say, all other participants can gain if any person works harder or saves more than his or her naked preferences might dictate. If my earlier arguments are accepted, there are mutual gains to a trade, of sorts, that might be worked out among all the participants. But think how difficult it would be to organize a formal contract of exchange in such a setting. Each person would be required to agree to work harder and/or save more if all others in the economy agreed to do the same, which is surely a contract that is almost unimaginably complex and impossible to enforce if made. Transaction cost barriers clearly rule out any such complex trade, despite the mutuality of potential gains.

The welfare economists of midcentury would have turned their attention to prospects for politicized action in the presence of the potential failure of exchange agreements. But the whole enterprise of welfare economics foundered on the selfsame grounds that rule out the exchange or contractual alternatives. In any broadly democratic politics, individuals must choose among the alternatives confronted, even if they are aware that they are choosing publicly or collectively rather than individually. But any "politicized contract" that might emerge from the interplay of interests in a democracy would surely be far too simple to secure more than a share of the potential gains that effective internalization of economic interdependence might offer. Politicized correction for the failure of explicit exchange or market arrangements to capture economic value that might be possible on behavioral shifts along appropriately defined margins of individual adjustments suffer from the implied universality in application. The fact that if any participants are to be encouraged to shift behavior, then all participants must be similarly encouraged, will, in itself, tend to inhibit the implementation of political actions.

We are left, almost as if by default, with ethics as the only viable means of capturing the potential economic value that lies over and beyond that which is secured by the workings of ordinary markets and ordinary politics (see Buchanan 1991). And a major advantage of ethical internalization of the externalities involved in the choices of persons to work and to save lies in the elementary fact that ethics are not contractual. There is no quid pro quo, as in political or economic exchange. Any participant in the economy is made better off, economically, if others work harder or save more, and the same applies to all participants, but there is no requirement that if others do save more or work harder, the reference person must follow suit.

Recognition of economic interdependence does, however, present each participant with an incentive to change, if possible, the behavior of others. And if the contractual processes of both political and economic exchange are precluded, the natural outlet for such incentive is investment in those institutions that embody attempts to modify behavior noncontractually. Each participant has, in this sense, an incentive to pay the preacher, even though free-ridership may emerge here as with all publicness relationships. In this section, we have derived a logic of ethics from the rational choice calculus of participants in an economic nexus, each of whom recognizes that his or her economic well-being depends on the behavior of others and that this interdependence extends beyond the limits of ordinary contractual institutions.

IV. PREFERENCES FOR PREFERENCES

I suggested earlier that the origins of ethical constraints stressed in this chapter are strictly economic. Persons have economic interests in the behavior of others with whom they socially interact, and they will act to further these interests, through investment in the institutions of socialization and acculturization. At this basic level of analysis, we need not depart at all from the standard economists' model of inquiry. We can examine the choice behavior, both actual and potential, of a person whose preferences are assumed to be exogenously determined. That is to say, at this level of inquiry, we do not require that a person exhibit a "preference for his or her own preferences," with some view toward reforms aimed at becoming a "different" person, as defined by preferences. As noted, all that is required is that a person exhibit a preference ordering over the preferences of others.

Such a stance seems descriptive of any person's complete ordering of all possible states of the world. Each of us is concerned about the preferences, the utility functions, of others than ourselves. And to say this is not to say that each of us has "meddlesome preferences" (Sen 1976). I can remain totally indifferent as among your preference orderings over alternatives, so long as your choices among these do not affect my economic well-being. But I cannot rationally remain indifferent to your preferences if your choices do, indeed, affect my economic well-being.

The analysis here becomes problematic only as we move to a second state at which the model is generalized to apply to more than one person at a time. If I am, indeed, interested in your preference ordering among potential choice alternatives, you will, similarly, be interested in my own orderings. And whereas it seems quite straightforward to postulate that my preference ordering is exogenously determined and not subject to my own higher-level choices, we cannot extend the exogeneity to imply that my preferences are totally immune to influence by others than myself. If we generalize the model to this extent, then any attempt to invest resources in changing the choice behavior of others must fail. The productivity of all such investment is zero, by presupposition, if preferences are not subject to change.

Economists become uncomfortable when analysis goes beyond the fixed preferences postulate, and most of the economists' research program, inclusively defined, embodies either explicit or implicit acceptance of such a postulate. Economists leave the domain of inquiry into preference formation to their peers in the other social sciences.

Ordinary sense observation suggests that the economists' stance in this respect is violative of reality. At best, the economists' model can be defended only on some principle of methodological reductionism. Persons do not simply emerge full blown with well-defined preference orderings over all potential alternatives for choice. As members of the human species, persons have biologically determined needs that are not socially endogenous, but even here the translation of these needs into preferences among alternatives that might be presented for choice may allow for widely divergent patterns. And once we move beyond strict biological limits, the range over which preferences may vary as among persons and within the life cycle of the same person covers a whole spectrum.

It seems plausible to suggest that preferences may be treated as "relatively absolute absolutes" for much ordinary analysis, but we also acknowledge that preferences may, themselves, be modified in the process of socialization and acculturization that describes the operation of the whole social environment in which a person is born, grows, and continues to live. To adopt this position on preference formation is not at all equivalent to accepting the arguments of modern communitarian philosophers and critics of economic analysis, who suggest that individual preferences are totally malleable and depend exclusively on the social environment. To acknowledge the influence of feedbacks between the social environment and preferences is not to deny either the individuality of persons, as defined by their preferences, or the relative imperviousness of such preferences to environmental influence.[6]

In sum, it becomes rational to pay the preacher only in settings that depart from the strict economists' model of fixity in preference orderings, but the productivity of investment in preference modification may fall well below that which is implied in the communitarian alternative.

V. BUT SOME NORMS ARE "BETTER" THAN OTHERS

Let it be acknowledged that we have a rational interest in the preferences of others with whom we interact if their choices affect our economic well-being, and let it also be acknowledged that, within limits, preferences can be changed by investments in the institutions of

[6]Herbert Simon has introduced "docility," which he defines as the "disposition to be taught," in an imaginative model that counters the orthodox proposition to the effect that nonaltruists must become dominant in the evolutionary process. See Simon (1990).

socialization. The logic of the economic argument for paying the preacher seems unassailable.

When, however, we move beyond the general analytical argument and attempt to apply the result to the institutions that we might actually observe, new difficulties arise. As should be obvious from the discussion, not all of the preference modifications that the preachers might induce are directionally consistent with our economic interests. Clearly, some classification must be made here; we should, indeed, all pay the preacher but only if he preaches that which upholds and furthers our economic interests. (Whether or not we might want to pay the preacher on other grounds is outside my scope of discussion.)

It is observationally evident that not all of the ethical-moral teachings that describe the pronouncements of our preachers, loosely defined to include moralists and educators of many shapes and sizes, qualify for our support under this logic. In chapters 1 and 2, I discussed the work and the saving ethics in these terms, and I suggested that we all secure spillover benefits from hard work and saving by anyone and everyone in the economic nexus. We should, therefore, be willing to invest something in support of all those preachers who shout out these virtues from their pulpits. Much the same logic, perhaps of a simpler and more universally accepted sort, could be extended to apply to those familiar precepts that call for honesty in dealings, for promise keeping, for truth telling, for respect for person and property, for sobriety, for tolerance. In short, we could readily include the whole set of constraints summarized within the rubric "the Puritan virtues." If we could but limit our preachers, of all stripes, to preaching these virtues, we should have no qualms at all about the social (economic) productivity of their activity, even if we also recognize that some of their preaching works its effects on us as well as on our neighbors.

Alack and alas, however, our preachers, our moralists, whether institutionally licensed or self-proclaimed, do not restrict their teachings to such old-fashioned rules for prudence. These preachers also urge us to have compassion for and be charitable to the less fortunate, even to the extent of selling what we have accumulated and giving to the poor, to join the wretched of the earth in their claims against the productive, to cease the pursuit of economic value, to take the time to smell the flowers, to use the coercive powers of politics to protect the wilderness against economic exploitation, to assist the efforts of political majorities in the exaction of tribute from those members of the minority who do, indeed, practice the Puritan virtues. The listing could, of course, be extended. But it is, or at least should be, clear that successful preaching along these dimensions may be unproductive and may actually reduce value in the economy. That is to say, we may be made worse off, in our own terms, if our preachers successfully cause our fellow participants in the economy to modify their behavior in accordance with the non-Puritan set of moral norms or constraints.

The upshot of all this is, yes, there are good, hard-headed economic reasons why we should support the institutions that are designed to modify the norms that serve to constrain the opportunistic behavior of participants in the economy, but it is essential that we be discriminatory in our investment. Here, as elsewhere, we should invest only where the promised returns are greatest and are, at a minimum, positive.

VI. PRAGMATIC BEHAVIOR AND ECONOMIC UNDERSTANDING

I have classified many of the moral norms often deemed to be praiseworthy as economically unproductive. But let me emphasize once again that these arguments are presented as exercises in economic explanation and not as ethical discourse. To say that there are economic reasons why persons should support institutional efforts designed to modify behavior in some ways but not in others is not to deny the existence of noneconomic origins of morals. And also note that my argument does not address prescriptive issues concerning how any particular person "should" or "ought" to behave. The argument says nothing at all about whether or not an individual should work harder, save more, tell the truth, or keep promises. The argument says only that the individual, any individual, will be "better off," in terms of economic well-being, if others work harder, save more, keep promises, and so on. And it is the recognition of this sort of interdependence that makes it privately rational to pay the right sort of preachers.

Or does it? Suppose that my argument in these respects is totally convincing. An individual recognizes the economic origins of ethical interdependence. But how can the effort, or investment, of a single participant in a large production-exchange nexus affect the wider standards of behavior of the whole community, other than in some minuscule amount? Recognition of the vanishingly small relationship between individualized behavior and collectively determined outcomes makes it difficult to bring cooperative behavior of many varieties within the explanatory model of rational choice. In large-number electorates, individuals do not find it economically rational to vote, and if they do vote, they find it rational to remain ignorant. In public goods interactions, individual beneficiaries do not find it rational to contribute, despite the excess of aggregated benefits over costs.

The free-rider logic would seem to apply here to possible individual investment in paying the preacher, that is, in supporting the institutions that are designed to modify behavior patterns in the ways that will allow for at least some internalization of the positive economic externalities that ethical interdependence ensures. The individualized act of paying the preacher would, in this argument, remain irrational, this despite the recognition of the externalities that might be efficiently corrected.

To an extent, we do find empirical evidence that individuals behave "irrationally" in some of the familiar large-number interactions that present the cooperative dilemma. Individuals do vote, and some of those who do vote try to become informed about the alternatives. Individuals do contribute toward the costs of publicly shared goods, even in situations where contributions are strictly voluntary. It is important to recognize, however, that there also exists an active ethical discourse that encourages individuals to surmount the large-number cooperative dilemma in such cases. Persons are encouraged to get out and vote, to become informed, and to contribute voluntarily to all sorts of public goods projects.

By contrast, to my knowledge, there exists little or no ethically directed, economically motivated argument that encourages individuals to work harder, to save more, to hold, generally, to the Puritan virtues, except in those pockets of our cultural heritage that have resisted the thrust of modernity. Should we be surprised, therefore, when we observe the non-Puritan moral norms emerging to replace the Puritan?

Perhaps criteria of strict rationality do dictate that others pay the right preacher. But criteria of understanding should inform us all that, in the cooperative solution, we should all pay the right preacher. And the absence of such understanding must be laid squarely on the shoulders of the economists, who have separated economics from its initial moorings as a part of moral philosophy. As I noted earlier, orthodox economic analysis has no place for recognizing much of the ethical interdependence among participants in an economic nexus, no grounds for appreciating more than the minimal role that moral constraints on behavior can play in generating economic value. Until and unless economists bring their "science" back into its proper relation to ethics, we can expect little generalized encouragement for paying the preacher, and of the right sort.

VII. MAX WEBER, CALVINISM, AND CAPITALISM

I have argued here that the set of attitudes summarized under "Puritan ethics" has been, is, and can be a major source of productivity in any economy that is organized broadly on market principles. The scope of my enterprise here and elsewhere prompts comparison with the well-known earlier efforts of Max Weber as represented in his widely acclaimed, if highly controversial book, *The Protestant Ethic and the Spirit of Capitalism* (1930), first published in German as early as 1904–1905 but only published in English translation in 1930.

Weber was a social and economic historian who sought to explain the origins of the capitalist or enterprise economy. Why did capitalism emerge in Europe, and where and when did it emerge? Weber's controversial thesis was that the capitalistic spirit, the spirit of enterprise, was intimately connected with the particular strand in Protestant theology (Calvinism)

that removed magic from religion, that placed emphasis on occupational calling, that made work and saving
behavior demonstrative of predestined selection rather
than some part of an exchange with the deity or his
earthly agents, that made accumulation and intergenerational transmission of wealth praiseworthy rather than blameworthy. This attitudinal stance was associated with the Calvinists, who stressed the sterner
requirements of Christianity rather than the gentler
and more personal requirements suggested in alternative theological constructions.

Critics were quick to challenge Weber's thesis on
several grounds, and they suggested, in particular,
that, as an empirical proposition, the Weber thesis was
readily falsifiable.[7] The spirit of capitalist enterprise
seems to have emerged in economies and in parts of
economies that exhibited little or no relationship to
Calvinism, Protestantism, or Puritanism. The notable
modern examples are, of course, Japan and the rapidly
developing Pacific Rim nations, where something akin
to Puritan ethics seems omnipresent in personal attitudinal and behavior patterns.

It is not my purpose here either to defend Weber or
to join forces with his many critics. My enterprise is
much more limited than his. I am neither competent to
trace nor interested in tracing the wellsprings of economic progress as these may be attributed to the
influence of this or that particular strand of theology,
whether Protestant, Catholic, Jewish, or Confucian.

[7]For one of the most careful criticisms, see Samuelsson (1961).

However, my enterprise may be considered to complement that of Weber, in the following sense. My thesis is that, regardless of its origins, in theology or elsewhere, the set of attitudes that Weber identifies has been, is, and can be important in generating and maintaining economic progress. A society whose members share the Puritan virtues, no matter what the source and for what reason, will be economically more successful than the society in which these virtues are absent or are less widely shared. Weber would not have disagreed; indeed, he started with the "givens" that my argument defends.

My own enterprise, in its relation to Weber's, can be illustrated by an imaginary tale. Suppose that John Calvin and/or some of his Calvinist followers reckoned that individuals could be moved to action only by theological persuasion. And, further, let us suppose that Calvin and/or the Calvinists had sufficient self-confidence to think that by advancing a new interpretation or new slant on existing theological constructions, a change in the set of attitudes along with consequent behavioral changes could be produced. In this setting, as imagined, Calvin and/or the Calvinists might have asked, What set of attitudes, and behavioral changes therefrom, is most desired? My suggestion here is that the answer to such questions might well have been "that set of moral-ethical norms that later generations will come to subsume under 'Puritan ethics.'" I do not, of course, suggest that either Calvin or the Calvinists were so crassly motivated as my tale implies; mine is an "as-if" tale, and it should be understood as such.

VIII. ECONOMICS AND ETHICAL INTERDEPENDENCE

The thesis that I have developed here may be summarized in the statement that individual participants in an economy are ethically as well as economically interdependent and that the moral constraints that may inhibit strictly opportunistic responses to choice alternatives are important in determining the value potential of that economy. So stated, the thesis seems almost self-evident, especially to those whose mind-sets are not immunized by the intricacies of modern economic theory. And even the most highly sophisticated theorists would not deny that an economy in which persons seize each and every opportunity to defraud trading partners will be less productive than an economy in which persons, for the most part, are honest in their reciprocal exchange dealings. Beyond these acknowledged limits, however, the sophisticates in modern economic theory back off; they will have no truck with the elementary notion that to work hard and to save are moral qualities that are analogous to honesty and promise keeping.

For those who are not scientists in the discipline, the argument is much easier to accept. If someone works harder, earns more, and spends more, the exchange network is expanded, and the general relationship between the size of the network and the well-being of all participants may seem more or less a natural one. For the economists, however, the relationship is not at all evident, and the preliminary response to my proposition is to deny its validity. If a person works harder (or saves more), he or she receives the full value of the addition to product that the behavioral change generates. How are other participants in the economy affected at all? I addressed this question in chapters 1 and 2. If I have been successful, I should have brought the economists around to an acceptance of what may seem to be ordinary commonsense reasoning to those who remain outside the scientific boundaries.

In this chapter, I have examined some of the implications of the recognition that economically relevant ethical interdependence extends beyond the minimal limits of honesty in exchange. If I am correct, if an economy in which participants are constrained by what we call "Puritan ethics" is indeed more productive, it follows as a matter of course that there are purely economic reasons for trying to instill or imprint this set of norms in all persons who may participate in the network of production, distribution, and exchange.

Let me emphasize, however, that the argument here is not one that sets up some external criterion, whether this be economic growth, economic efficiency, or anything else, with the view toward promoting the moral-ethical norms that would indirectly further the achievement of this objective. I am not to be interpreted as suggesting that ethical norms may assist in maximiz-

ing some social welfare function. As in my other
works, the methodology here remains strictly individualistic. Hence, when I suggest that there are economic reasons for the transmission of ethical precepts (for
paying the preacher), I refer to reasons that apply to
each and every person in the inclusive economic nexus.
We are all in this together, and each and every one of us
faces essentially the same situation.

I shall, indeed, be better off if everyone else abides
by that set of moral precepts that ensures economic
progress, but all of you, reciprocally, will be better off
if I, too, adhere to roughly the same set of moral
norms. Finally, the argument from ethical interdependence does not depart from a basic contractarian logic
of sorts, even if the explicitly contractual elements in
the ethics that inform our behavior may be lost from
consciousness.

PART II
THREE PAPERS ON THE THEME

The three chapters part II comprises are separately developed applications and extensions of the basic analytical argument advanced in part I. The inclusive principle is that the interdependence among participants in an exchange or market nexus is not fully captured in the economists' stylized models of competitive structure, even in the absence of the familiar sources of market failure.

Chapter 4 contains the most straightforward analysis in the book. The beyond-market interdependence among participants in an economy that is created by the necessary presence of a tax-financed public or governmental sector is examined in some detail. The fiscal interdependence here is, of course, almost universally recognized. But the precise implications for the ethical norms that may describe the behavior of persons, either as taxpayers or as public program users, are not nearly so widely understood and, indeed, are seldom explicitly discussed.

Both chapters 5 and 6 are exploratory inquiries that are, perhaps, more controversial than those introduced elsewhere in the book. The economics of the work ethic was introduced in chapter 1, but "work" was, at least implicitly, limited to labor, the human input into production. Chapter 5 extends the logic to nonlabor resources, and the argument suggests that any "idleness" in resource use must exert negative effects on participants in the whole interaction nexus. The behavior of owners in using nonlabor resources in this way or that becomes in itself ethical to the extent that other persons may be affected by the marginal shifts in the size of the market nexus.

To work more, to save more, and to use nonlabor resources productively — these potential choices all affect the size of the inclusive market and, through this, the extent of specialization that is potentially exploited. Chapter 6 goes beyond the possible direct effects of resource-using choices on market size and introduces possible indirect effects of within-market choices on the extent of possible specialization. To "work harder" is to "demand less leisure," and leisure can, for many purposes, be treated as a "good," even if nonmarketable. But to demand more or less of *some* marketable goods-services may exert comparable effects. Menial services are examined in this context. The results suggest that Adam Smith's distinction between productive and nonproductive labor, which has been almost universally dismissed as misleading and erroneous by economists, may have economic relevance, at least as applied to menial servitude.

Chapter 4

Externality in Tax Response

PREFATORY NOTE

This chapter reprints without major change an article
that was published two decades prior to the full development of my interest in the economics of ethical norms.
The central point made in the chapter, however, can be
placed within the inclusive analysis of ethical interdependence developed in other chapters of this book. In a
general sense, of course, the extra-exchange economic
interdependence discussed under the externality rubric
in welfare economics can simultaneously be treated as
extra-exchange ethical interdependence.

Reprinted with some changes from *The Southern Economic Journal* 33, no. 1
(July 1966): 35–42. The article originated as a digression from a general
analysis of the effects of tax institutions on individual behavior in political
process. For the latter, see Buchanan (1967).

The analysis here is simpler and more direct than that in other chapters of the book. If participants in an economy are linked through the taxing-spending process, they become ethically interdependent quite apart from the presence or absence of increasing returns. A person has a measurable economic interest in others' payment of assigned tax shares even if there is no change in the productivity of inputs as the size of the economy increases.

I. INTRODUCTION

Theoretical welfare economics and theoretical public finance should be closely related fields of inquiry. Specifically, the implications for changes in behavior that stem from the Pigovian and post-Pigovian analysis of external economies and diseconomies should find some application in the discussion of tax institutions and in proposals for tax reform. Surprisingly, the bridge between these two areas has not been fully developed, and results that seem obvious have not been noted. Theoretical welfare economics has been developed largely on the assumption that a public sector of the economy does not exist, while theoretical public finance has continued to embody a serious neglect of the essential two-sidedness of the fiscal account. If these defects in both models are removed, the theorems of Pigovian welfare analysis can be extended directly to the web of fiscal interdependence that the very existence of a public sector normally introduces.

The notion of externality has been central to Pigovian welfare economics. The fundamental theorem is that when individual actions impose relevant external effects on parties outside a marketlike contract, the necessary conditions for Pareto optimality are violated. Recent contributions have clarified the policy implications of this theorem, notably, its relation to what has been called "market failure" (Coase 1960, Buchanan and Stubblebine 1962). The point to be noted here, however, is that, almost exclusively, the discussion of externalities has been confined to individual decisions or actions taken in the private sector on the assumption that a public sector does not exist. In an earlier paper, I traced some of the simple implications of the externality aspects of individual behavior as a participant in public choice (Buchanan 1962). I shall not be concerned with such collective-choice behavior here. The analysis is confined to individual choice in the market or private sector of the economy but under the plausible assumption that a public sector exists and that familiar institutions of taxation are used to finance public goods and services. The fiscal structure in this setting introduces complex interdependencies among individuals' behavior as they respond to tax changes by modifying their market choices.

I shall not be concerned with the normative problem of deriving the necessary marginal conditions for optimality in public goods supply. I assume, realistically, that public goods are financed through the familiar institutions of taxation that embody little or no attempt to relate individual marginal evaluations to individual marginal taxes. Most of the discussion will be limited to income taxation, although extension to other taxes is straightforward.

The analysis to be developed is closely related to but also quite different from that which has carried the label "excess burden" to scholars in public finance. Well-known theorems here state that any tax that causes individual behavior to be different from that which would prevail under the imposition of lump-sum levies generates an "excess burden," an "unnecessary" welfare loss that could be eliminated if the same revenues should be collected through the lump-sum alternative. The ideally efficient tax, in this context, is the lump-sum tax that, by definition, exerts no substitution effects; this is normally used as the benchmark for measuring the relative efficiency of alternative tax institutions.

The feature that distinguishes the analysis here from the traditional excess burden discussion lies in the sharply different political setting for the two models. Implicitly, excess burden analysis assumes that taxes are collected from the economy in complete independence from the financing of public service benefits. By contrast, I shall assume that taxes are collected solely for the purpose of financing public service benefits that are enjoyed by the same set of persons as those who pay the taxes.

Let us now examine somewhat more specifically the results attained in the externality and the excess burden discussions before introducing the variations. The whole policy emphasis of the Pigovian literature is placed on the relative desirability of encouraging marginal extension in the output of those activities that exert relevant external economies and of encouraging marginal contraction in output of those activities that exert relevant external diseconomies. Recent contributions have raised questions about the efficacy or even the possibility of accomplishing these desired ends through any simple or straightforward instruments of policy (e.g., taxes and subsidies), and, also, they have emphasized the necessity of comparing the institutional processes carefully before recommending specific policy actions (Davis and Whinston 1962). The underlying logic of the central theorem has not, however, been essentially modified, and, within all of the necessary limits, the economist who is called on to provide policy advice would surely recommend against public or governmental measures that clearly encourage persons to behave in such a way as to impose external diseconomies on each other.

Consider now the familiar results of the standard excess burden analysis applied to a single tax institution, say, proportional income taxation. Because the individual is led, by the introduction of the tax, to substitute nontaxable income (e.g., leisure) for taxable income, his or her utility is reduced to some level below that which could have been maintained under an equal yield lump-sum tax, because the latter, by definition, generates no substitution effects. Note that the emphasis here has been almost exclusively on the welfare losses suffered *by the individual who is taxed*.

This is accomplished through the equal yield assumption under which the comparative analysis has always been conducted. If equal revenues are collected from an individual under either of two tax alternatives, the positions of others in the community remain the same under either of the two. Somewhat strangely, or so it now seems to me, no one has examined the prospect that the behavior of the individual, at the margin of adjustment, may be imposing Pareto-relevant externalities on his or her fellow taxpayer-beneficiaries. In responding to any nonefficient tax levy, the individual acts so as to reduce the tax base. It may be, and normally will be, to the advantage of others, as a group, to work out compensations with the individual in exchange for an agreement on his or her part to limit his or her base-reducing behavior. Therefore, even if others are totally unconcerned with the "excess burden" or welfare loss that the nonefficient tax imposes on the individual himself or herself, they may find it in their own interest to "trade" with the individual with respect to his activity that imposes the external diseconomy. As a result of such trades, the individual will contribute more to the public treasury than the comparable equal yield taxes allow.

The analysis here seems complex only because of the arbitrary restrictiveness imposed by the equal yield assumption. Once this is dropped and individual behavior in response to the levy of a single nonefficient tax is examined, the relationship becomes clear. As a result of the imposition of the tax, say, a proportional income tax, the individual acts so as to reduce taxable income. The aggregate tax base for the revenue is reduced. Necessarily, all citizens in the group who are simultaneously taxpayers and public service beneficiaries are harmed. To secure the same quantity of public services as before, tax rates must be increased. Or, conversely, at prevailing rates of tax, the level of public benefits must fall. The precise distribution of external diseconomies among individuals as taxpayers and as public goods beneficiaries depends, of course, on the rules through which the two sides of the fiscal account are tied together. If the budget is fixed and tax rates must be adjusted residually so as to produce the necessary revenues, the tax response of an individual in reducing taxable income does not impose external diseconomies on his or her fellows who are beneficiaries but not taxpayers. In this case, the diseconomies are limited to his or her fellow taxpayers. However, if tax rates are fixed and the budget is residually determined, the tax response of the individual generates external diseconomies only for individuals in their capacities as beneficiaries and not as taxpayers.

The interdependence becomes less direct when government borrowing is introduced, although the basic effects are not changed. If government borrows so as to maintain a constant level of public service supply in the face of revenue-reducing behavior, individuals need not experience current spillover harm. Insofar as they anticipate the future taxes that will be required to service and amortize the debt, they will suffer current reductions in utility. If they fail to capitalize future taxes, because of some fiscal illusion, the external diseconomy involves individuals as future, not current, taxpayers.

Before examining some of the implications that the recognition of this quite evident interdependence involves, it will be interesting to discuss briefly why it has been largely absent from the standard analysis of taxes. As suggested, most tax analysis has been based on a conceptual separation between the two sides of the fiscal account. If, in fact, taxes represented net drainages from the economy, of the sort aptly labeled as *imposte grandine* by Luigi Einaudi, no external effects of the sort described above would arise, provided, of course, that the amount of revenue collection is not predetermined. In this sort of model, the behavior of the single taxpayer in reducing the tax base in response to some nonoptimal levy does not affect, in any way, the position of other taxpayers in the political group. And in such a model, there are no public service beneficiaries since there are no public goods financed. The welfare loss from the nonoptimal tax is concentrated strictly on the person who is led by the tax to change his or her behavior, and there are no spillover effects of his or her action on others. The external diseconomy arises only in a model that imposes the essential two-sidedness of the fiscal account.[1]

[1]The interdependence will be present in all models that incorporate both sides of the budget account except for the extremely restrictive one in which the demand for public goods is directly related to the amount of taxable income earned and to nothing else. In this model, an individual's decision to reduce taxable income reduces the aggregate tax base, but, at the same time, it reduces

The question is, of course, whether or not the *imposte grandine* model is at all relevant for analyzing fiscal institutions in the real world. I have argued that it is not and that it is necessary to incorporate the interdependence between taxes and benefits in any analysis claiming applicability. Individuals, as participants in democratic decision processes, directly or indirectly, impose taxes on themselves to provide public goods to themselves. In this fundamentally democratic model of political activity, the externality that is inherent in tax response must be recognized.

II. IMPLICATIONS FOR POLICY

At one level, the analysis here does little other than to supplement and to strengthen the familiar efficiency of excess burden theorems. The nonoptimal tax imposes a welfare loss on the individual who responds directly but, also, and because of his or her response, on other members of the community. The incidence of nonoptimality is more diffused than is implied from orthodox fiscal theory. But there is more to it than this relatively straightforward extension. As recent contributions have made clear, the existence of relevant externalities will, necessarily, set up situations that

---

the demand for public goods. In any reasonable model, some relationship between public spending needs and the amount of taxable income earned in the economy probably exists, but this seems only to reduce somewhat the particular interdependence discussed here, not to eliminate it. (I am indebted to Francesco Forte for this point.)

make further "trades," "exchanges," or "rules changes"
profitable to all affected parties. In small-number
groups, individuals suffering damages from external
diseconomies imposed by the behavior of others can
directly initiate arrangements through which they
offer appropriate compensations in exchange for some
contraction in the scope of the activities in question. In
the large-number group, the free-rider phenomenon
arises to make individual initiation of direct action
unlikely, but unexploited "gains from trade" here may
be secured from general agreement on changes in the
rules through which activities are allowed to take
place.

In examining tax responses, it is appropriate to
limit consideration to the large-number case; fiscal
jurisdictions normally include many citizens. This
suggests that pressures for the reduction or elimination
of externalities in tax response may not spontaneously
emerge from the private initiative of individuals but
that widespread agreement may be forthcoming on
properly designed modifications in the rules that gov-
ern interpersonal interaction. As some of the recent
contributions have indicated, however, small-number
models may be useful in deriving constitutional-insti-
tutional changes to be presented in large-number
settings.

Consider an extremely simplified two-person model, which we use solely as an analogue to a large-
number model. It is to be assumed that some previously established "constitutional" rule, binding on the

collectivity, requires that public goods, which are shared equally by both citizens, be financed by the levy of a proportional tax on personal incomes. In the absence of any tax, individual A will earn an income of $1,000 per period, and individual B will earn $500. Now assume that a collective decision is made to finance the purchase of three units of a public good, at a cost of $50 per unit. The precise rule through which this collective decision is reached is not relevant for our analysis; it is specified only that the decision, once made, is binding on both citizens. If both persons earn their pretax incomes, a rate of 10 percent will finance the chosen quantity of public goods. A would pay a total tax bill of $100, and B would pay $50.

Some allowance for individual response to the imposition of the tax must, however, be introduced. Suppose that individual B finds it almost impossible to substitute nontaxable for taxable income, whereas individual A can make such a substitution with relative ease. Let us say that in response to a prospective tax rate of 10 percent, individual A will reduce his taxable income receipts to $500. He will do so, let us say, by working only one-half as much as before, taking his nontaxable psychic income in the form of added leisure. The tax levy of 10 percent would now produce revenues of only $100, and this would finance only two units of the public good, not three. To finance the additional unit, the rate of tax must now be increased, or the collectivity must accept the shortfall in quantity. Clearly, A's behavior in response to the tax, his or her action in reducing taxable income from \$1,000 to \$500, imposes an external diseconomy on B. This diseconomy may be measured in terms of B's evaluation of the third unit of public good, if we assume that the shortfall is to be accepted. In one sense, of course, A also imposes an "external" diseconomy on himself, in his role as a beneficiary of the public good. However, this aspect of A's action may be left out of account; this would not influence his own behavior in a large-number setting, and, recall, we employ the two-person here only as an analogue of the large-number case.

Recognizing that A's anticipated response to the imposition of the tax will exert a diseconomy on him, B will find it advantageous to look for means to persuade A to act differently. Assume that B values the third unit of the public good at \$10. He would, therefore, be willing to offer, as compensation to A, any amount up to \$10 in exchange for some agreement on A's part not to reduce taxable income. In the context of this example, some bargaining range is clearly present, and some agreement should emerge which would be advantageous to both parties. Independent of any offer of compensation, A's behavior reveals only that he prefers the alternative (1) \$500 taxable income under the tax, to the alternative (2) \$1,000 taxable income under the tax. His behavior, or predicted behavior, does not reveal whether he prefers, say, \$500 taxable income under the tax to, say, \$1,005 under the tax. His elasticity of substitution between taxable and nontaxable income may be very high.

Let us presume that some bargain is struck. In exchange for a $5 payment from B (which for numerical simplicity we shall assume is nontaxable), individual A agrees to earn taxable income in the amount of $1,000. Net of tax, therefore, A will now get $900 plus $5, or a total of $905, whereas B will receive, net of tax and compensation paid to A, $445. For the three units of public good that can under this arrangement be made available to both persons, A has paid a net tax of $95, while B has paid a net tax of $55. The rule of proportionality to income is violated. But as the example clearly demonstrates, both members of the group have benefited from the departure from strict proportionality; both persons are better off than they would have been under simple proportional income taxation without compensation. Individual B, in the bargain, pays more than a proportionate-to-income share in the costs of the public goods, but he is better off by so doing because, in the bargain, he secures a larger supply of public goods. In the absence of "trade," B gets two units of public good for $50, or a "tax-price" per unit of $25. With trade, he secures three units for $55; his tax-price falls to $18.33.

The numerical example is, of course, quite an arbitrary one. The roles of the two persons in the model could as well have been reversed. If B, with the lower income, finds it more convenient to substitute nontaxable for taxable income than does A, then a departure from proportionality in the opposing direction, in exchange for some agreement on the part of B to earn more taxable income, would be indicated. The general result of the model should, nonetheless, be clear. If individuals differ with respect to the opportunities and the tastes for substituting nontaxable for taxable income, some mutually advantageous "exchanges" involving individual tax responses and appropriate compensations are likely to be possible.

III. ILLUSTRATIVE PROPOSALS FOR REFORM

How might this general result be applied to the reform of tax institutions? Individuals are not, of course, classified exogenously by the elasticities of substitution between taxable and nontaxable income. If some means could be found to determine just what each person would earn in potentially taxable income in the absence of taxation, then these data could be used to determine, ideally, the allocation of taxes among persons. Of course, no such means exists. What is required seems to be some institutional recognition of the direction of the fiscal interdependence that is present. Certain steps toward this objective may be suggested.

The example in the preceding section, as well as most of the general discussion, concentrated on the external diseconomy that the individual's change in behavior imposes on his fellows. This diseconomy stems from his response to the imposition of a tax, a response that involves the reduction in the aggregate tax base. The obverse relationship among individuals is equally obvious. In the face of an existing tax structure, a change in an individual's behavior in the direction of earning a higher taxable income, hence expanding the aggregate tax base, exerts an external economy on his fellows. Institutionally, recognition and reward for changes in behavior that exert such external economies may be more readily introduced than recognition and penalties for changes in behavior that exert external diseconomies.

I propose here to examine only one suggestion for possible reform in some detail. No attempt is made to explore other possible steps in reforming tax institutions to incorporate some recognition of the fiscal interdependence analyzed here. Let us suppose that the existing personal income tax is changed so that individuals are taxed not on measured taxable income in the year t, the period during which the income is earned, but instead are taxed, in year t, on income that is earned in the year $t - 1$. In this case, the individual whose income increases from Y_{t-1} in year $t - 1$ to $(Y_{t-1} + \Delta Y_{t-1})$ in year t, is allowed the increment (ΔY_{t-1}) free of tax. In this extreme, of course, other members of the political group receive no gain from the decision made to increase income; no external economies are exerted here since other taxpayer-beneficiaries secure no gain via the fiscal interdependence process. In this extreme, the individual who earns the income increment is allowed to secure all of the potential gains-from-trade that the interdependence generates. However, at any tax rate on the income increment greater than zero, such spillover benefits do accrue to other taxpayer-beneficiaries. This suggests that a more appropriate institutional change may be one that imposes some tax on the income increment — but at some rate less than the maximum marginal rate on base income. For simplicity, think now of the individual as being subjected to a rate equal to one-half of his maximum marginal rate on the increment to income. This change alone would clearly provide individuals with a strong incentive to increase taxable income through time.

Note especially that such a proposal for change in the personal income tax need not be subject to the standard criticism concerning a reduction in progressivity of the system. The rate structure, which could be applied to base or standard income, could be regressive, proportional, or progressive at whatever scale the community desires. What is required here is that this standard or base rate structure, applied to income in the period immediately past, be supplemented by a second rate structure applicable only to income increments. If the measure of income for applying the base rate structure is that earned in year $t-1$, individuals who suffer income reductions would, of course, be worse off than under current-year assessment. To some extent, such differentials might be considered as appropriate penalization for the genuine external diseconomies that are imposed. However, consideration should perhaps be given to those individuals whose income reductions are largely fortuitous. This suggests a modification of the proposal. The individual may be allowed a choice as to the base year for determining income for tax purposes. He can choose between (1) the base rate structure applied to income earned in the current period, t, and (2) the base rate structure applied to income earned in the period $t - 1$, plus one-half of the maximum marginal rate applied to the income supplement, the difference between income in $t - 1$ and income in t. Those persons whose income increases over the two periods will, of course, always choose the second alternative. Those whose income decreases over the two periods will choose the first alternative, which is, of course, the standard current-period income tax.[2]

In an economy characterized by increasing aggregate income, a large share of the population will, of course, experience personal income increases through time. To the extent that individuals would have earned higher incomes through time, apart from any change in income tax, the differential reduction in marginal taxes represents an "unearned reward." No such "institutional bargain" need be made to secure the increments to income in this case. However, the proposal

_____

[2]Protection might have to be provided against deliberate income reduction aimed at securing tax advantage. Under the unqualified option rule suggested, the individual has some incentive to reduce income in t, to exhibit income growth between t_1 and t_2, and because of this, a lowered marginal rate of tax in t_2. This potential loophole might be closed effectively by disallowing the differentially lower marginal rate on recovery-growth in income to some trend path. Again, I emphasize that the analysis is intended for illustrative purposes, and I am not primarily concerned with the possible virtues or defects of the proposal as a practicable scheme for tax reform.

will surely have the effect of causing some individuals to increase their earnings of taxable income over time. Since these two shares in incremental personal income cannot be effectively distinguished, any decision to introduce proposals along the lines suggested would have to be based on some balancing of the two; some estimate of the net change in income growth that the proposals would induce must be made. To the extent that aggregate income growth, in and of itself, is considered to be an important policy objective, quite apart from the fiscal interdependence elements stressed in this chapter, additional and supplementary argument is provided for the introduction of the change that has been suggested. The effects would surely be some increase in the rate of aggregate income growth in the economy.

In this strict sense, the change would violate horizontal equity in the tax if the criterion for equality among persons is defined as equality in present values for future income streams. The individual whose pattern of income earnings over time starts from a low relative base would be subjected to a lower tax (also measured in present-value terms) than the individual whose present value of future income is identical but whose time pattern of earnings exhibits less growth. This does not seem to provide a formidable objection to the proposal. When problems of comparing different time patterns of income are introduced, the question of just who are equals among taxpayers seems largely open.

The existing social consensus with respect to vertical equity among income classes need not be changed by the proposal. The change introduces differential rewards to those persons whose incomes increase through time, not to those whose incomes are "high" or "low" at particular points in time. Note, however, that this reward or compensation stems from a recognition of the essential interdependence of the fiscal structure and not on some exogenously postulated objective such as "growth," although, as mentioned, the acceptance of such an objective can provide supplementary support. The interdependence suggests that the introduction of the proposal could benefit not only those whose incomes rise over time but also those whose incomes are not expected to rise. The latter secure benefits because of the external economies that income growth generates via the fiscal mechanism. Properly conceived, some such change can be, in itself, Pareto optimal in the sense that all persons in the group can either be made better off or left undisturbed. This is not, of course, the same as saying that the position attained, after the change, would be Pareto optimal, globally considered.

IV. CONCLUSIONS

The discussion has been limited to one specific illustrative proposal that would embody some recognition of the fiscal interdependence among separate members of the taxpayer-beneficiary group. Other, more elegant, proposals might be made. What is required is some differentially favorable treatment for individual behavior that exerts "fiscal" external economies and/or some differentially unfavorable treatment for behavior that exerts "fiscal" external diseconomies. The proposal suggested uses the temporal pattern of income to distinguish base-period from incremental income. Some such arbitrary device seems necessary to prevent undue conflict with norms for vertical equity in modern tax systems. Even for single-period models, however, explicit modifications in progressivity may, in certain cases, prove worthy of consideration because of the arguments that have been advanced. Vertical equity norms should be balanced against other values. Some reduction in the rate of progressivity may prove beneficial, even to those who stand to pay a higher proportionate share of their own income as a result. Some implicit recognition of the externality here has perhaps been present in the orthodox discussion of the effects of taxation on incentives. The externality analysis explicitly makes it clear why the incentive effects are important, even to those in groups that are not directly able to modify income-earning patterns and even if the growth objective is overlooked.

The argument can be applied to other suggestions for fiscal reform. A case for differentially favorable tax treatment of the incomes of working wives is provided here, wholly apart from equity considerations. Similarly, income earned in moonlighting, in overtime, and during holiday periods can be treated as supplementary income, and it may become advantageous for *others* than those who earn such incomes to grant differentially favorable treatment to such incomes.

As suggested several times, the central point of this chapter is an extremely simple one. The man who sits on his sunlit patio when he could be earning taxable income is levying costs on his fellows. The man who labors and thereby earns taxable income when he could be sitting in the sunlight is providing his fellows with benefits. Discussions for fiscal reform should explicitly recognize the existence of this interdependence.

Chapter 5

The Economics and the Ethics of Idleness

I. INTRODUCTION

In this chapter, I want to concentrate attention on idleness in the use of potentially productive resources, particularly on the ethical aspects of individuals' choices concerning the margins of productive employment. This subject matter has been neglected in modern microeconomic analysis, which has embodied the presumption that potentially productive resources will be employed optimally, within the constraints faced by individual resource owners, so long as the choice of employment is voluntary. The whole Keynesian macroeconomic emphasis, which came to occupy the atten-

A somewhat different version of this chapter was initially presented as the Henry George Lecture at St. John's University in November 1990.

tion of economists in midcentury and did have profound political impact, was centered on involuntary unemployment, or, to use my terminology in this chapter, on idleness that is not chosen to be preferred by resource owners. Furthermore, the modern emphasis of economists, to the extent that they have concerned themselves at all with idleness in resource use, has been almost exclusively confined to labor; little or no attention has been given to possible idleness in the utilization of nonlabor resources, the primary subject matter here.

It is necessary first to define idleness, which I do in section II. I then proceed, in section III, to show that there are ethical implications of individual choices in resource utilization. Initially, I develop the analysis in application to labor or work input, an application that was developed in chapter 1. In section IV, I briefly sketch the outlines of an argument to the effect that voluntary choices made by resource owners need not be such as to generate economic efficiency in the standard sense, an argument that directly counters the conventional wisdom in economic theory. In section V, attention is shifted from labor to nonlabor resources. Finally, in section VI, some interesting policy implications are suggested that seem to follow from the whole exercise.

II. IDLENESS DEFINED

Precisely what do we mean when we say that a resource, or resource unit, remains "idle"? We define idleness by its opposite; a resource is idle when it is not "at work," when it is not "employed." More generally, we can say that a resource is idle when it is not being used to produce value that it might otherwise produce. Such generalized understandings are satisfactory for most purposes, but they are not sufficiently specific for my purposes here.

Note, in particular, that the definition suggested could be used in application to the activities of Robinson Crusoe, all alone on his island and totally outside any nexus of interaction, economic, political, or social, with other human beings. Crusoe may, of course, work hard and employ his own talents and time to produce something of value to himself. In some descriptive sense, we could measure Crusoe's idleness as distinguished from his work. But his choices in this respect could not carry ethical content since there are no others who could possibly be affected. And Crusoe might, for example, spend his time and energy, his "work," building sand castles that are swept away by each evening's tides.

I want to introduce a more useful meaning of idleness by opposing this use of resources to "work in an interactive relationship with others" or "employment in producing value for others." In this more restricted but more useful definition, a person is idle when and to the extent that he or she withholds work effort from the market, even if, on some "private island," nonmarketable sand castles are constructed. A resource, or resource unit, that can produce value when placed on the market but that is withheld from the market or from production for own use by the owner, which allows consumption purchases on the market to be replaced, is *idle*. The subjective value that may be produced for the resource owner is irrelevant.

I also want to rule out of consideration any non-voluntary idleness in the use of resources. Involuntary idleness may be important in many settings, but this sort of idleness is not my concern here. For the analysis and discussion that follows, I shall presume that all owners of resources may, if they choose to do so, place such resources in employment by way of sale on the market. There exists a parametric price per unit of resource supplied to the market, and the owner-supplier may adjust amounts to this price, from zero to some employment maximum (or idleness minimum).

As noted, I initially develop the argument in application to labor, but I do not restrict the analysis, as such. Idleness can characterize the utilization of any resource, labor or nonlabor, no matter how classified. I shall make the appropriate extensions as required. There are differences between labor and nonlabor resource units that are worthy of notice, however, differences that offer some explanation of economists' concentration on labor. The presumption is that for any nonlabor resource, under the assumption that resource owners face parametric prices in the market, voluntary choices will always lead to maximum resource utilization, or, stated conversely, to minimum idleness. I demonstrate that this conclusion does not follow if we are careful to remain with the definition of idleness stated above.

III. IS IT UNETHICAL TO LOAF?

Consider a simple example, in which we initially neglect the fiscal interdependence considerations treated in chapter 4. There is a highly trained, professionally competent radiologist who is, at age forty-five, at the height of his career. He can secure an income of $200,000 annually. In January 1994, this person chooses, voluntarily, to work no more. He opts for the life of leisure; he "retires"; he lives off his accumulated savings, plays golf and tennis, and enjoys society. He undertakes no further productive effort. Henceforth, he remains idle.

How would this choice be evaluated by the modern economist? The forgone payment of $200,000 would have reflected, in some rough-and-ready sense, the net contribution to value in the economy that was made by the radiologist. The value of the national economic product will fall by this total on the radiologist's choice to retire. But the economist would also note that the $200,000 also measures the preretirement income received by the radiologist. Hence, the person who makes the choice between productive work and idleness bears the full burden of payment. No one else in the national economy is affected, at least in any directly measurable economic sense. The choice made by the radiologist is the same as if he were, indeed, a Robinson Crusoe on his private island. There seems to be no ethical content in this choice, no ethical implications that result, because others find themselves in the same positions whether or not the radiologist chooses work or leisure.

There are some necessary qualifications to this conclusion. First, as the discussion in chapter 4 makes clear, if taxes are levied on measured money income, then the choice made by anyone to earn less income and to take more leisure will reduce public goods benefits and/or increase taxes on others in the fiscal system. I shall simply acknowledge the effects of this fiscal interdependence here; I shall neglect further discussion because I do not want to base my central argument on this point. Second, if resources are specialized, as is always the case for transitional periods, the change in relative prices will generate gains for some groups and losses for others. In some long-run sense, however, these effects disappear, and, under the conditions presumed necessary for a workably competitive economy, the primary conclusion seems to stand up. There seems to be no important spillover effect on others that stems from the choice made by one income earner, even a high-income earner, to loaf rather than to continue to supply productive effort to the economic nexus.

This apparent result squarely contradicts one of the first principles of economics, a principle first enunciated clearly by Adam Smith in 1776. There exist mutual gains from trade; all parties gain from exchange, and these gains increase with extension in the size of the trading network. As the network of exchange expands, increasing advantage emerges from the increased specialization that is made possible. What has happened when the radiologist in our example decides to work less is that the market has been reduced in size. There will be less prospect of fully utilizing the advantages of division of labor, at least for some area of production in the economy. There will be permanent changes in the price vector for outputs; inputs will earn less than before; the purchasing power of an input in terms of potentially purchasable output will fall. If this hypothesis holds, then the choice made by the radiologist in the example does, indeed, exert spillover effects on others in the whole system of interaction. This choice on the part of one person will necessarily harm others in the system. And if harm to others is the criterion for unethical or immoral behavior, the choice to loaf rather than to continue to offer productive work to the economic nexus can legitimately be classified as unethical or immoral.

IV. INCREASING RETURNS

Here as well as in earlier chapters, I have exposed what I consider to be a rather glaring contradiction between two parts of the conventional wisdom in modern economics, a contradiction that seems to have been largely, if not completely, overlooked. The tone of my discussion in the preceding section, as well as earlier in this book, conveys my own analytical preferences, so to speak. I want to argue in support of the basic principle that all members of the inclusive production-exchange-consumption nexus tend to secure gains as the effective size of this nexus expands and that these gains are inexhaustible. That is to say, increases in specialization are always possible as markets are extended, producing, in turn, increases in economic well-being for participants.

But acceptance of this principle requires that the standard conditions for the attainment of equilibrium in a competitive economy be modified in some way. The vulnerable assumption in the model of competitive adjustment is that which postulates that, at equilibrium, firms operate everywhere in the range of constant returns to scale of operation. Note what happens under this postulate. In our simple example, the radiologist chooses to work no more. The competitive adjustment process ensures that, after a transitional period, the price of radiology services will return to the same level as that prevailing prior to the decision made by the single supplier to cease productive effort. The services previously provided by the man who chooses to smell the flowers will now be generated by some expansion in the scale of operation of other radiologists or by the entry of newly trained professionals. In either case, after the gains and losses over the transitional period are damped and a new equilibrium established in the industry, the first result identified emerges. The choice between idleness and productive effort on the part of any input supplier does not permanently affect the economic well-being of others.

To generate a result consistent with the inexhaustible gains-from-trade story, we must allow for the presence of increasing returns (decreasing costs) to the size of the economy. In our example, the size of the measured nexus is lower by $200,000 annually compared to what it was before the shift in preferences on the part of the person in question. Somewhere in the system, at some or all locations, in some or all industries, there are now specialist producers or suppliers, of some inputs or some outputs, who find that the market faced is no longer sufficient to allow previously established patterns of trade to remain viable. Production is forced into a higher-cost mode of operation because the market will no longer support the specialization attained under the extended market. There will be an increase in the real price of the products or services that are ultimately produced. The shrinkage in the size of the economy will have required resort to an "inferior" technology, relative to that which was supportable before the change.

V. THE IDLENESS OF NONLABOR RESOURCES

To this point in my argument I have introduced analysis and material that I have discussed differently and in somewhat more detail in earlier chapters. I now propose to enter uncharted territory, to extend the same analysis to apply to nonlabor resources. It is relatively straightforward to discuss the choice between idleness and productive effort in application to labor. The picture becomes cloudy when nonlabor resources are treated. In my radiologist example, it is meaningful to think about the shift in preferences that caused the person to cease supplying productive effort to the marketplace and to supply, instead, hours of leisure to himself. There is nothing incoherent about a utility function that shifts in such a way as to make this choice take place. Leisure, or the uses to which leisure may be put, yields utility values to the individual, values that must, in all cases, be compared with those that emerge from the ultimate purchasing power over consumable goods and services that income received from the sale of productive work effort makes possible.

But what is the equivalent to the utility value of leisure for nonhuman resource units? Recall that we must always remain within an individualistic calculus of choice here. Resource units do not, in themselves, take on characteristics that allow us to attribute values directly to them. We must remain with the utility calculus of those persons who own and control the utilization of nonhuman resource units. But why should an individual, as owner-supplier of a nonhuman resource unit, secure any potential utility value from withholding this unit from the market nexus?

It is relatively straightforward to understand why the owner of a resource unit would place such a unit on the market. The resource unit, if it is productive, yields a market price that provides the owner with income that may be used for the purchase of desired goods and services from other markets. But why should such an owner ever choose to withhold or to withdraw a unit from the marketplace?

For this result to occur, idleness in resource use must yield direct utility to the owner, analogously to that yielded by leisure to the supplier of potential work effort. Again, consider an example. A person accumulates under his personal ownership and control several thousand acres of marginally productive agricultural land. This land is leased or rented to farmers who produce and market crops. The lease or rental value to the owner is $10,000 annually, which is approximately the value of the increment to product attributable to the land itself. The owner receives the $10,000 in annual rental value and returns this value to the income stream in either consumption goods purchases or indirect investment in capital goods.

Let us now assume that the owner of the land experiences a shift in preferences concerning the usage of the land. He chooses voluntarily to withdraw the land from active production of crops and to utilize this resource in its natural state, say, as a hunting preserve. The land becomes idle, in my usage of terms here. To the owner, the choice can be fully rational; the owner withdraws the land from production for the market in the full knowledge that he or she is sacrificing $10,000 annually in rental or market value. The utility value now placed on the idleness of the land must be anticipated to yield more than the utility yielded by $10,000.

The example seems in all respects analogous to the labor-supply example of the radiologist discussed earlier. The inclusive economic nexus is made smaller by the decision of the landowner to withdraw the resource from production for the market. A market value of $10,000 could be produced with the resource, but this value is now replaced with a utility yield that is enjoyed exclusively by the owner of the resource. Other persons in the production-exchange-trading nexus are placed in a less-preferred position due to the shrinkage in the size of the market. The smaller economy will be unable to allow for the full exploitation of the scale advantages that the potentially larger market might make possible. Some of the benefits of specialization will be lost.

If work is praiseworthy and loafing is blameworthy; if there is positive economic content in an ethic of work, as I have argued in chapter 1 and elsewhere, then there must also be comparable normative implications for the employment of nonlabor resources. If nonlabor resources are capable of producing value on the market, or value that is a direct substitute for goods that would otherwise be purchased from the market, there are external or spillover effects of decisions made by resource owners concerning the way in which these resources are used.

Note that the emphasis here is not explicitly distributional, although distributional implications may be derived indirectly. In our example, the owner of the land does not exert a negative externality on others in the polity because he has extensive holdings. The negative externality stems exclusively from the owner's

use of the holdings, from the withholding of potentially productive resources from the market nexus.
Indeed, it is the owner's decision to forgo measured
money income, the rental value of the land, that
imposes the costs on others. Because the owner does
not earn this income and return it to the economy's
circular flow as effective demand, the gains-from-trade
that might otherwise be possible are not exploited.

VI. IMPLICATIONS

Recognition of the ethical content present in choices
between placing resource units on the market and
withholding them in idleness does not imply that there
need be some all-or-none commitment. Recognition
that the radiologist, in the first example, does indeed
provide spillover benefits to others in the economy as
he produces value that he, in turn, spends for his own
purposes, does not allow us to infer that the radiologist
is immoral if he supplies anything less than the physi-
cally determined maximum number of hours of work.
Additional work supply involves disutility to the supplier, and this decrement to value must be measured
against (1) the utility value of the income earned to the
radiologist, plus (2) the spillover value to others in the
nexus. Beyond some point, the disutility of additional
work surely offsets the value, both internal and external, of this work, even in some idealized felicific
calculus. The point of my whole discussion here is to
stress that there should be some recognition given to

the value to others than the work supplier in the choice made between productive effort and idleness.

Much the same logic applies to the landowner's choice in the second example. The landowner does indeed impose costs on others in the economy as he withdraws land from the production of marketable value. But there need be no normative inference to the effect that land, or any other nonhuman resource, should always be utilized so as to yield maximal marketable product value. The hunting preserve presumably yields utility to the owner, and this utility (like leisure to the worker) should not be left out of account. Again, the point to be noted is only that the effects on others than the choice maker, the landowner in this example, should not be overlooked.

I have argued that it would be extremely difficult, if not impossible, to internalize or correct for resource use externalities by ordinary economic or political adjustments. I suggested that such internalization that exists enters the calculus of choice makers by way of ethical constraints, which may or may not be conscious to the choosers. The radiologist may feel guilty when he does not work, and the landowner may feel a guilt of sorts when he converts the land into a hunting preserve.

Recognition of the interdependencies discussed can, however, lead to agreement on institutional changes that will, at the least, remove perverse incentives. The potentially useful changes are perhaps most evident in tax policy. The radiologist who chooses to forgo income for leisure should be required to pay *more*, not less, in taxes. Yet, as we realize, most tax systems that are based on income would allow the radiologist's tax liability to be reduced as the income earned in the market falls. In this respect alone, the substitution of a consumption or expenditure base for an income base of tax would represent a major welfare-enhancing step. The landowner of our second example, who withdraws land from productive use to a purely private use, should be required to pay higher, not lower, taxes in any fiscal system that embodies a conceptually agreed on structure of incentives.

As we move beyond fiscal incentives, perhaps the most serious distortions in incentives are to be located in the failure of effective decision makers on resource use to be confronted with relevant opportunity costs, even to the extent faced by genuine resource owners in our two examples. At the very least, both the radiologist and the landowner make choices to withdraw resources from the market in the full knowledge that they will, privately and personally, suffer the loss of measured product value. In many cases, however, and especially in the modern economy-polity, resource use decisions are made by political agents, presumably acting on behalf of citizens. And these agents do not face the incentives of the marketplace at all. The coalition in the legislature that approves the withdrawal of productive land for preservation of "wilderness areas" or "wildlife habitats" loses neither the direct opportunity cost of lost market value nor the spillover harms generated by the necessary reduction in the size of the inclusive trading nexus along with the effects of the lowered tax base. If public policy analysts could incorporate the elementary principle that "resource use matters" for the ultimate size of the market, some corrective offset to the modern prejudice against the production of market value might be introduced.

Let me end with a private, personal story. In May 1989, I visited Prudhoe Bay, on the Alaskan North Slope, where I toured the oil-producing facilities. Let me state categorically that there could be no place more desolate than this North Slope in the absence of facilities—a barren, frozen, uninhabitable desert. There exists another section of the North Slope that is anticipated to yield oil, but development has been prevented because of the misguided and confused judgment that such pristine wilderness should be preserved. This judgment is, to my mind, grossly immoral and especially so in that those who pronounce such judgment, and who do, indeed, exert political influence, do not stand to suffer any of the adverse consequences of the smaller economy that must result as we fail to take advantages of our resource-using opportunities.

The main thrust of my argument has been that the market, as it operates, does not fully take into account the advantages of production for the market because some share of these advantages accrue to other than those who make choices directly. But the argument is strengthened manyfold in application to politics, where those who make ultimate resource-using decisions share almost none of the costs of the sacrifice of opportunities that are forgone.

Idleness for private aesthetic purposes comes at a cost that even the hard-nosed economists have not properly reckoned. Should we be surprised at all by the relative decline in the productive record of the U.S. economy after the flower children of the 1960s came to work and the romantic environmentalists mounted their efforts to make us return to a natural state? Idleness is idleness is idleness, no matter what the dross.

Chapter 6

The Simple Economics
of the Menial Servant

I. INTRODUCTION

Adam Smith made much of the distinction between
productive and unproductive labor, and the ratio between these categories of employment was a central
determinant of the wealth of a nation. This ratio
provided a rough measure of the extent of the market,
which, in turn, set limits on the potential for the
division of labor. And, as Helen Boss notes, "Adam
Smith's Scottish soul is particularly troubled by the
'unproductiveness' of menial servants" (Boss 1990: 47).
Neoclassical economics does not incorporate the pro-

The central argument of this chapter was initially presented at a seminar at
George Mason University in February 1991, and it was again presented at the
Southern Economic Association meeting in Nashville in November 1991.

ductive-unproductive labor distinction, and the conventional wisdom attributes analytical error to Smith in this aspect of his general argument.

My purpose here is to suggest that perhaps it is neoclassical economists generally who are in error and that Smith's argument may be made coherent on careful and critical reinterpretation. I shall demonstrate that, under conditions to be specified, the participants in an economy may be "better off" in terms of their own revealed preferences in settings where they collectively discourage the purchase of personal services of others, in the capacities of menial servitude. My analysis is limited here to what we may call the "welfare economics" of menial servitude rather than the more familiar relationship between the productive-unproductive labor ratio and classical theories of economic growth.

II. THE EXTENT OF THE MARKET

Smith's distinction between productive and nonproductive labor must be analyzed within the context of his overreaching principle to the effect that the division of labor is limited by the extent of the market. Modern economists, with a small but rapidly growing number of exceptions, have by and large paid lip service to the central Smithean proposition here, while proceeding to ignore its implications almost completely in their analysis. The Smithean principle suggests, quite simply, that any extension or expansion in the size of the market or production-exchange nexus will necessarily allow for an increase in specialization, which must, in turn, increase the overall productivity of the resource inputs that are devoted to generating outputs for such nexus. By inference, there is no upper limit to this potential for specialization.

Economists have been able to ignore the implications of the Smithean proposition here because they have postulated, either explicitly or implicitly, that the quantity of resources is exogenously fixed. That is to say, the "size of the market" is not within the choice set of participants in an economy, either individually or collectively. Given such a postulate, it is not surprising to find that Smith's principle has been more fully discussed and understood by those economists who analyze problems in international trade.

But, of course, the postulate of resource fixity is absurd. The quantity of input supplied to the market or production-exchange nexus is a choice variable, within the choice set of individuals, either as they adjust privately and independently to the constraints they face or as they participate variously in collective decisions for the group, as they may or may not impose constraints that will be faced jointly by all or some participants. To postulate fixity in the supply of the most important input, labor, to the market is to carry forward the exploitation thesis that workers are required by subsistence limits always to maximize the hours of employment and/or to accept the more sophisticated utilitarian fallacy that classifies nonwork (leisure) as a "good" that is analytically equivalent to market input.

Clearly, the extent of the market can be expanded endogenously by choices made by participants to supply more inputs to the market and fewer inputs to themselves, in nonmarket uses. As individuals supply more inputs to the market nexus, specialization is increased, and the productivity of inputs increases. The quantity of outputs, appropriately measured, that is purchasable from any given input is increased.

From this straightforward analysis, it follows that the supply of inputs that will be forthcoming under individualized adjustment to input prices (wages) as if these prices are parameters will be suboptimal. There will exist an external economy in input supply, at the work-leisure choice margin, an externality that will not be exploited. All persons in the economy can be made "better off," by their own evaluations, by some modification in the constraint set that will offer incentives for an enhanced input supply.

I have discussed this labor supply externality more fully in chapter 1, and I shall not elaborate earlier arguments here. But a different formulation of the work-supply externality analysis will be helpful in moving toward the central argument of this chapter with reference to the unproductiveness of menial servitude.

III. A SIMPLE MODEL OF LABOR SUPPLY WHEN THE EXTENT OF THE MARKET MATTERS

Consider an economy in which all persons are identical, both in their preferences and in their capacities or endowments. In this setting, there would be no trade under the standard neoclassical assumption of constant returns of scale of production for each good. Trade will prove beneficial only if there are increasing returns to specialization, which I assume to be present. Further, I assume that the gains to specialization are not exhaustible, no matter what the extent of the market.

Specialization takes the form of the replacement of general purpose or multipurpose inputs by newly specialized inputs that enter into the production of final goods.[1] There are many goods in the economy, produced with many inputs. The valued bundle of goods that is produced and marketed may be measured in units of an all-purpose numeraire consumable unit, X.

Smith's principle states that X is produced under increasing returns from the supply of inputs. For simplicity, assume that labor is the only input and that the amount of labor supplied to the market is Z. Then X, the all-purpose consumable, is produced under increasing returns to Z.

Persons have available a fixed number of potential labor inputs, measured by total time available (24 hours per day). Since, by assumption, all persons are identical, if all behave in the same way, each person would confront a nonconvex production possibility set. Such a production possibility frontier is depicted by the curve P in figure 1, where hours (Z) are measured on the abscissa and income (X) along the ordinate. The individual will not, however, be aware of the gener-

[1] In this respect, the model is similar to that introduced by Ethier (1982).

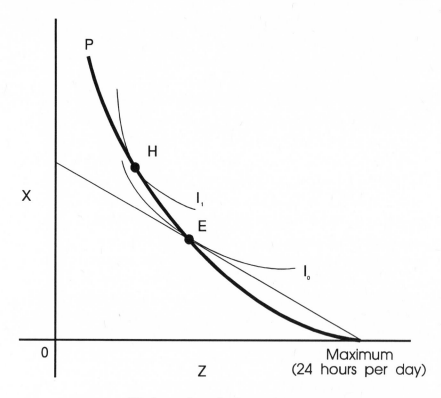

FIG. 1. Work supply under increasing returns

alized increasing returns present in the economy. If the economy operates competitively, each person will confront an apparent transformation set that reflects a fixed wage rate, which is determined independent of the individual's choice. The competitive equilibrium adjustment is shown at *E*, where the individual's (all individuals) marginal rate of substitution between labor supplied to the market and income (through the wage rate) is equal to the apparent possibility constraint and where the solution falls somewhere on the real set of production possibilities.

It is clear from the construction in figure 1 that E, the competitive equilibrium, is nonoptimal. The individual (all individuals) may be placed in a position of higher utility if the solution could, somehow, be shifted to H, where the marginal rate of substitution between work supply and the wage is equal to the real rather than the apparent marginal rate of transformation. (This result can be easily understood if we think of a setting where a single individual, in a one-person economy, faces the situation depicted. Utility maximization would dictate a location of equilibrium at H, not at E.) In the competitive adjustment equilibrium, there is a suboptimal supply of labor to the market nexus and a supraoptimal supply of labor to the nonmarket uses, including leisure.

This result is derived independent of any prospect for defining, in advance, the good or goods in the market that are produced under increasing returns of the standard sort. The result suggests that the supply of labor input is suboptimal so long as the basic Smithean principle concerning the extent of the market is accepted, that is, so long as the gains from further specialization remain unexhausted. The result emerges exclusively from the elementary fact that specialization, hence increasing returns, cannot be extended by the supply of inputs to nonmarket uses, that is, to the "production" of nontradable "goods."

Once the use of potential labor market input for nonmarket purposes is recognized and the necessary absence of gains from specialization in "producing" for such purposes is acknowledged (specialization could not conceivably extend beyond each person's use of his own leisure), the nonoptimality of individualized parametric adjustment to exogenously determined wage rates is evident.

Note that the construction indicates that the range of suboptimality in the supply of market input is limited. In chapter 1, I have suggested that one means of internalizing the externality here is through the inculcation of a work ethic, which operates as a constraint of preferences. Note that such an ethic that might expand work effort beyond that point depicted at H in figure 1 would, in itself, be overly constraining.

IV. IDENTIFICATION OF "GOODS" THAT CANNOT BE PRODUCED UNDER INCREASING RETURNS

The analytical conclusion of the previous section hinges on the identification of input use that cannot give rise to increasing returns; this procedure is the reverse of that which characterizes much of modern welfare economics, where the attempt is made specifically to identify input uses that generate increasing returns. And the approach here seems more in keeping with the Smithean emphasis, especially with the emphasis of Allyn Young (1928), who, in his seminal paper, associated economic growth with increasing returns but made no attempt to identify, in advance, the industries where specialization would generate relatively greater benefits.

If leisure, or own-consumption use of inputs, can be identified as a utility-enhancing "good" that cannot possibly generate increasing returns and, indeed, may generate the opposing effect through reducing the overall size of the market or exchange nexus, some further search for other valued "goods" that might be comparable in this respect to own-consumption uses of own inputs might be suggested. And it is only here that I return to the economics of menial servitude, the primary subject matter of the chapter.

Consider, now, the same simple model as previously analyzed, but assume that one of the valued goods in the X bundle is personal service. Persons in the economy have preferences such that services provided by others enter as arguments in utility functions, again assumed identical for all persons in the economy. Personal services differ from nonwork or leisure, however, in that these services are directly tradable; they are marketable "goods" that persons sell and purchase through the market or price system.

As before, we incorporate acceptance of the basic Smithean principle concerning the effects of extending the market. We postulate that there are increasing returns, generally, as measured in units of X, with increases in the supply of Z. The composite consumable, X, is, however, now made up of two categories of "goods," personal services, X_s, and all other "goods,"

X_{ns}. Can we now argue that inputs used to produce X_s cannot give rise to increasing returns, comparable to the results applied to leisure or nonwork earlier?

V. PERSONAL SERVICES AS SUCH

It seems evident that if care is taken to specify precisely what personal service or menial servitude means in the context of the model analyzed here, we can indeed add such service to the putative listing of "nonproductive" labor, which we have essentially redefined as that labor which cannot possibly generate increasing returns. At least two qualifications must be placed on the type of personal services that fall under the classification suggested here. First of all, the use of inputs for personal service may substitute for own-service in nonmarket purposes and, in the process, provide scope for extension in the effective size of the market. A household example is familiar. A person may, through the purchase of the personal services of someone else (e.g., services for care of children), have more time available for supply of his or her own inputs to the market nexus, inputs that are valued more highly than those replaced by taking the services supplied by the employee from the productive nexus. A second qualification involves the possibility that personal services may be supplied only in a package with other inputs that may, indeed, generate increasing returns and, in the process, give rise to a reduction in the personal service component of the final consumable. Haircuts may offer an example here. Barbering services are required to supply haircuts, but these personal services are supplied jointly with other technical equipment services. As the market for haircuts increases, increasing resort to the technical equipment components (e.g., electric clippers) in the jointly supplied "good" may increase the productivity of the complementary personal inputs of the barber. The result may be that the time spent per haircut is reduced, indicating the presence of generalized increasing rather than constant returns.

I suggest, however, that these are qualifications on the general Smithean claim and that they do not seriously undermine the validity of the proposition. To the extent that labor inputs are used to provide personalized services, as such, to others, even as fully valued and paid for on competitive markets, these inputs are used unproductively relative to those uses that might give rise to increasing returns consequent on specialization. If I purchase, for a full market wage, the services of a menial servant, whose work for me in no way makes me a more productive input supplier to the marketplace and whose work is not supplied jointly with some nonpersonal input components, I am, in taking this choice, reducing the relevant extent of the market, as measured in terms of its potential exploitation of gains from specialization. Clearly, the extreme limits of specialization are reached when one person does nothing other than provide personal services for another. The productivity of this sort of input cannot possibly be enhanced by any widening of the market nexus.

The construction of figure 2 is structurally identical to that in figure 1, but here the trade-off depicted is that between X_s, personal services, and other goods, X_{ns}. Since we have postulated that there must be increasing returns to Z, the input of labor services to the whole economic nexus, as measured in X, the numeraire consumable, there must be a nonconvex real possibility frontier between personal services and other goods, as shown by P^1 in figure 2. The individual who faces exogenously determined competitive prices will, however, be unaware of the generalized trade-off and will adjust to the solution shown at E^1. The solution is suboptimal in that the preferred solution at H^1 remains within the possible. Conceptually, all persons could be brought into agreement on the imposition of institutional constraints that would cause the solution to shift toward H^1 and away from E^1.

We may conclude, I think, that something more than Adam Smith's "Scottish soul," as named by Helen Boss, led him to classify menial service as relatively unproductive. His particular argument here may have been, instead, based on very solid economic analysis, even if he could not fully articulate his basic intuitions.

Note precisely what is being argued here. In earlier chapters, I have tried to establish the following proposition: If we accept the basic Smithean theorem that relates the division of labor and, hence, productivity gains from specialization to the extent or size of the market, and if, further, we acknowledge that the effective size of the market, as measured by the quan-

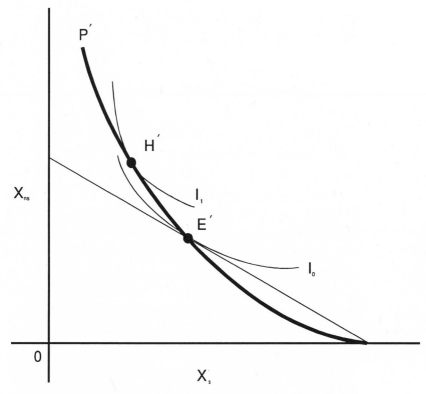

FIG. 2. Increasing returns to goods other than menial service

tity of inputs supplied, is endogenously chosen by participants, then it follows that individuals will not, in full competitive adjustment, offer optimal input supplies to the market at a level that will generate overall efficiency in resource use. The argument of this chapter is a direct extension of the earlier proposition but with an important difference. If we can identify valued uses of inputs that are intrinsically limited in their potential for allowing any exploitation of further gains from specialization, then acceptance of the Smithean theorem implies that a shift of demand from such "relatively unproductive" uses to other uses that might possibly allow for some exploitation of increasing returns will be welfare improving, quite independent of any overall adjustment in the supply of inputs to the market.

Note that the external diseconomy identified here is imposed by the person who uses income to purchase or demand the pesonal services of another person. The particular choice of a person to supply personal services is not, in this setting, different from a choice to work for a wage in producing goods. Again, as Smith noted, the shift of demand away from the services of personal servants or retainers and toward the purchase of goods became one of the means through which economic growth was made possible.

VI. BAUMOL'S UNBALANCED GROWTH MODEL REVISITED

To this point, I have restricted discussion to a single input use, the provision of personal services, as such, by some persons to others, even in a fully reciprocal and voluntary set of market exchanges. My concentration on this input use is prompted by a desire to evaluate Smith's particular attribution of relative unproductivity to this employment of labor. If my central argument is accepted, Smith's treatment is, in a sense, validated, despite the dominance of opposing arguments in the conventional wisdom of modern econo-mists. But if the argument is accepted, even provision-ally, the restriction of analysis to menial or personal service becomes arbitrary. An extension of effort to examine other input uses, including but not limited to Smith's listing, that may be classified to fall within the relatively unproductive category is clearly in order.

Perhaps surprisingly, given the apparent attitude of most modern economists toward the productive-un-productive labor distinction, we find that such an extended classification has been made but in quite another context and not explicitly related to Smith's extent-of-market theorem. I refer here to William J. Baumol's seminal paper, "Macroeconomics of Unbal-anced Growth" (1967). In his model, Baumol divided the economy into two sectors, distinguished by pre-dicted rates of growth in labor productivity. The sector characterized by constant or low growth in produc-tivity was defined to include those activities where "for all practical purposes the labor is itself the end prod-uct" (416). Examples were teaching, chamber music and orchestral performance, theatrical presentation, and fine cooking.

Baumol did not, however, relate his analysis to Smith's distinction between productive and unproduc-tive uses of labor, although it would have represented a simple step for him to assign those input uses de-scribed in terms of low productivity into a "relatively unproductive" category. Further, Baumol did not con-nect his analysis with the increasing returns sources of potential economic growth that Young had tried to initiate several decades earlier. Baumol's focus seemed to be primarily on the temporal dimension of productivity growth in his two sectors of the economy rather than on any quantitative dimension that might be measured by the relative sizes of the two sectors.

It now seems even more interesting that Baumol, himself a distinguished welfare economist, failed to draw any welfare inferences from his model. From the perspective of a quarter century later, it becomes possible to interpret Baumol's failure here in terms of the mind-set of neoclassical economics of the 1960s. The rate of economic growth was attributed to exogenous technological change that Baumol did, indeed, identify with particular sectors of the economy but that was not deemed to be dependent on the allocation of resources as between sectors. All productive activities were assumed to be characterized by constant returns to scale, and Smith's central theorem was relegated to the elementary textbooks. Operating from within this mind-set, Baumol's insights simply did not allow him to recognize that welfare-improving shifts from his relatively unproductive to relatively productive uses of resources were within the possible.

As we move now into the mid-1990s, the possibilities of economy-wide increasing returns are being reexamined (Kaldor 1985, Buchanan and Yoon forthcoming) and not only in international trade theory; classical theories of economic growth are being revived and reinterpreted (Eltis 1984, Reid 1989); theories of endogenous growth are on the frontier of economic analysis.[2]

Formalized definitions and existence proofs of the static allocative efficiency of competitive equilibrium occupy decreasing attention. Developments both in analysis and in observed reality force economists to recognize the interdependence among the economic, ethical, and political environments within which persons interact. During the last two decades, economists, generally, have learned that institutions matter. They must increasingly come to learn that ethics also matter. In both respects, we are returning to the classical tradition of Adam Smith after the Walrasian diversions of more than a half-century.

[2]See, in particular, the several important papers by Paul M. Romer (1986, 1987, 1990).

References

Baumol, William J. "Macroeconomics of Unbalanced Growth." *American Economic Review* 57 (June 1967): 415–26.

Boss, Helen. *Theories of Surplus and Transfer.* Boston: Unwin Hyman, 1990.

Buchanan, James M. "Politics, Policy, and the Pigovian Margins." *Economica* 29 (February 1962): 17–28.

———. "Ethical Rules, Expected Values, and Large Numbers." *Ethics* 76 (October 1965): 1–13.

———. *Public Finance in Democratic Process.* Chapel Hill: University of North Carolina Press, 1967.

———. "On the Work Ethic." In *Essays on the Political Economy.* Honolulu: University of Hawaii Press, 1989, 47–51.

———. "Economic Interdependence and the Work Ethic." In *The Economics and the Ethics of Constitutional Order.*

Ann Arbor: University of Michigan Press, 1991*a*, 159–78.

―――. "Economic Origins of Ethical Constraints." In *The Economics and the Ethics of Constitutional Order.* Ann Arbor: University of Michigan Press, 1991*b*, 179–93.

―――. "The Supply of Labour and the Extent of Market." Presented at the Adam Smith Conference, Edinburgh, Scotland, 1990, and in *Adam Smith's Legacy: His Place in the Development of Modern Economics*, edited by Michael Fry. London: Routledge, 1992, 104–16.

Buchanan, James M., and W. C. Stubblebine. "Externality." *Economica* 29 (November 1962): 371–84.

Buchanan, James M., and Gordon Tullock. *The Calculus of Consent.* Ann Arbor: University of Michigan Press, 1962.

Buchanan, James M., and Yong J. Yoon, eds. *The Return to Increasing Returns.* Ann Arbor: University of Michigan Press, forthcoming.

Coase, Ronald H. "The Problem of Social Cost." *Journal of Law and Economics* 3 (October 1960): 1–44.

Congleton, Roger. "The Economic Role of a Work Ethic." *Journal of Economic Behavior and Organization* 15 (1991): 365–85.

Davis, O. A., and A. Whinston. "Externality, Welfare, and the Theory of Games." *Journal of Political Economy* 70 (June 1962): 241–62.

Eltis, Walter. *The Classical Theory of Economic Growth.* London: Macmillan, 1984.

Ethier, W. J. "National and International Returns to Scale in the Modern Theory of International Trade." *American Economic Review* 72 (June 1982): 389–405.

Gauthier, David. *Morals by Agreement.* Oxford: Oxford University Press, 1985.

Hayek, Friedrich A. *Law, Legislation and Libery.* Vol. 3, *The*

Political Order of a Free People. London and Henley: Routledge and Kegan Paul, 1979.

Heiner, Ron. "The Origin of Predictable Behavior." *American Economic Review* 73, no. 4 (September 1983): 560–95.

Kaldor, Nicholas. *Economics without Equilibrium.* New York: Sharpe, 1985.

Levy, David. "Utility Enhancing Consumption Constraints." *Economics and Philosophy* 4 (1988): 69–88.

Reid, Gavin. *Classical Economic Growth.* Oxford: Blackwell, 1989.

Robertson, D. H. *Economic Commentaries.* London: Staples Press Ltd., 1956, 148.

Romer, Paul M. "Increasing Returns, Specialization and External Economies: Growth as Described by Allyn Young." University of Rochester, Rochester Center for Economic Research, Working Paper no. 64, December 1986.

———. "Growth Based on Increasing Returns Due to Specialization." *American Economic Review* 77 (May 1987): 56–62.

———. "Endogenous Technological Change." *Journal of Political Economy* 48 (October 1990): S71–102.

Samuelsson, Kurt. *Religion and Economic Action.* New York: Basic Books, 1961.

Sen, Amartya K. "Liberty, Unanimity and Rights." *Economica* 43 (August 1976): 217–45.

Simon, Herbert A. "A Mechanism for Social Selection and Successful Altruism." *Science* 250 (December 21, 1990): 1665–68.

Smith, Adam. *The Wealth of Nations.* New York: Random House, 1937.

Spencer, Herbert. *The Data of Ethics.* New York: A. L. Burt, n.d.

Weber, Max. *The Protestant Ethic and the Spirit of Capitalism.*
London: Allen & Unwin, 1930.

Young, Allyn. "Increasing Returns and Economic Progress." *Economic Journal* 38 (1928): 527–42.

Index

Altruism, 4

Baumol, William J., 142–44
Boss, Helen, 129, 140
Buchanan, James M., 7, 73; and W. C. Stubblebine, 93; and Yong
    J. Yoon, 144

Calvinism, 2, 62, 83–85
Capital: formation and saving, 45–51; productivity, 47
Capitalism and puritan ethics, 83–86
Circular flow, 124
Clark, John B., 20
Coase, Ronald H., 93
Communitarianism, 77
Competitive equilibrium, 6; and constant returns, 17–23, 119;
    optimality of, 6

Constant returns, 17–23, 119; and competitive equilibrium, 6;
    neoclassical economics, 6
Constitutional economics, 7
Constitutions as constraints, 65
Constraints: constitutions as, 65; ethics as, 1; contractarian origins
    of, 61, 65–66
Consumption taxes, 126
Contractarian origins of constraints, 61, 65–66
Cost, theory of value, 19
Criteria for evaluation of saving, 33–38

Davis, O. A., and A. Whinston, 95
Deficits and saving, 38
Distribution: in neoclassical economics, 18; in idleness, 123–24
Division of labor and extent of market, 6, 12–17, 130–32

Economic growth: endogenous, 145; and increasing returns, 6, 136–
    37, 144
Economic "science" and ethics, 83
Economics: constitutional, 7; of ethics, 1; of self-control, 61, 63–65;
    of servitude, 129–45; welfare, 72–73
Economies of scale, 25
Einaudi, Luigi, 98
Eltis, Walter, 144
Environmental choices: and incentives, 126; and opportunity cost,
    126
Ethics: as constraints, 1; economic origins of, 60–88; in economic
    theory, 5; and economic "science," 83; economics of, 1; erosion of
    saving, 54; and free riders, 79; and guilt, 8; and loafing, 116–18;
    Puritan, 2; Puritan and capitalism, 83–86; of saving, 3, 31–59;
    of work, 2, 5–30
Excess burden of taxes, 94–95
Extent of market: and division of labor, 6, 12–17, 130–32; and
    specialization, 119, 131

Externality: and increasing returns, 24–46, 118–20; Pigovian, 95; in Pigovian welfare economics, 93; in tax response, 91–111; in work-leisure choice, 6, 132

Federal Reserve System, 41
Flow, circular, 124
Free riders and ethics, 79
Future generations and saving, 34, 42–44

Goods, leisure as, 29–30
Growth: economic and increasing returns, 136–37, 144; endogenous economic, 145; unbalanced, 142–45
Guilt, and work ethic, 8

Hayak, Friedrich A., 63
Hobbes, Thomas, 13

Idleness: distribution in, 123–24; in resource use, 112–28; in resource use, definition, 113–14; as withholding from market, 115
Incentives for environmental choices, 126
Increasing returns, 6; and economic growth, 136–37, 144; and externality, 24–26, 118–20; and international trade, 144; and optimality, 24–26
Internalization of externality and work ethic, 26–29
International trade and increasing returns, 144
Involuntary unemployment, 113

Kaldor, Nicholas, 144
Keynes, John Maynard, 34, 39–41, 46, 54, 112; unemployment model, 113

Labor, productive and unproductive, 129–45
Leisure, 121; as a good, 29–30; and specialization, 136; and
    taxation, 126; work choice and externality, 6, 182
Loafing, and ethics, 116–18

Macroeconomics, 11–12, 34
Marginal productivity: and constant returns, 20; theory of
    distribution, 19–21
Marginal utility theory, 19
Market failure in welfare economics, 93
Market size, and specialization, 15
Marx, Karl, 18
Measure of work, 11
Meddlesome preferences, 75
Menial servants, productivity of, 129–30
Menial servitude and welfare economies, 130
Models: Keynesian, of unemployment, 113; Ulysses, 64; Robinson
    Crusoe, 46, 114, 116

Neoclassical economics, distribution, 18
Net drainage of taxes, 98

Opportunity cost of environmental choices, 126
Optimality: of competitive equilibrium, 6; and increasing returns,
    24–26
Origins of constraints, contractarian, 61, 64–65

Paradox: of saving, 39; of thrift, 39, 54
Pareto, Vilfredo, 24, 53, 66, 93, 96, 109
Philosophy, political, 7
Pigou, Arthur C., 92, 94; analysis, 92; models and externality, 95;
    welfare economics, 92–93
Political philosophy, 7

Preferences, 74–77; meddlesome, 75
Productive labor, and unproductive, 129–45
Productivity of menial servants, 129–30
Public choice, 7; and capital, 47; marginal, and constant returns, 20; marginal, and theory of distribution, 19–21
Puritan: ethics, 2; ethics and capitalism, 83–86; virtues, 79

Reid, Gavin, 144
Resource use: in idleness, 112–28; in idleness, definition of, 113–14
Returns to scale, 25
Robertson, D. H., 71

Saving: and capital formation, 45–51; criteria for evaluation, 33–38; and deficits, 38; ethic, erosion of, 54; ethics of, 3, 31–59; and future generations, 34, 42–44; paradox, 39; and taxation, 38; and welfare state, 54–57
Scale economics, 25
Self-control, economics of, 61, 63–65
Self-sufficiency, 13–14
Sen, Amartya K., 75
Servitude: economics of, 129–45; menial and welfare economics, 130
Smith, Adam, 6, 12–13, 15, 17–18, 22–23, 25, 90, 117, 129–45
Specialization, 14–15; and extent of market, 119, 131; and leisure, 136; and market size, 15
Spencer, Herbert, 32
Stubblebine, W. C., and James M. Buchanan, 93

Taxes: consumption, 126; excess burden, 94–95; externality, 91–111; and leisure, 126; net drainage, 98; and saving, 38
Theory of value, cost, 19
Thrift, paradox of, 39, 54
Transaction costs, and trade, 72

Unbalanced growth, 142–45
Unemployment: involuntary, 113; in Keynesian models, 113
Utility theory, marginal, 19

Virtues, Puritan, 79

Walras, Antoine A., 144
Weber, Max, 2, 62, 83–85
Welfare economics, 72–73; economies, and menial servitude, 130;
    and market failure, 93; Pigovian, 93
Welfare state, and saving, 54–57
Whinston, A., and O. A. Davis, 95
Wicksell, Knut, 20, 66
Wicksteed, Philip H., 20
Withholding from market, idleness as, 115
Work, measure of, 11
Work ethic, 2, 5–30; in economic theory, 5; and guilt, 8; an
    internalization of externality, 26–29
Work-leisure choice, and externality, 6, 132

Young, Allyn, 136, 144